SUSAN CAMPBELL
CAROLINE CONRAN

POOR COOK

ACKNOWLEDGMENTS

To Miss Emily Spencer for her experienced help in the kitchen, to Carol Amos and Patricia Moran for all kinds of patient work, and to many friends who contributed recipes.

SUSAN CAMPBELL
CAROLINE CONRAN

POOR COOK

CLEARVIEW BOOKS

Published in the UK in 2012 by Clearview Books
11 Grosvenor Crescent, London SW1X 7EE

Copyright © Caroline Conran Ink

First published by Macmillan in 1971

The right of Susan Campbell and Caroline Conran to be identified as the authors of this work has been asserted by them in accordance with the Copyright, Designs and Patents Act 1988.

All rights reserved worldwide. No part of the book may be copied or changed in any format, sold, or used in a way other than what is outlined in this book, under any circumstances.

A CIP catalogue record for this book is available from the British Library

ISBN 978-1 908337139

Cover and book design by Jojo Hastie Design

Printed in China

CONTENTS

INTRODUCTION

Everybody loves eating expensive food, but extravagant meals often mean crises in greedy households, and lead to eating cheap food which alas, needs far more care and attention to make it really good. Happily people who love cooking like the challenge of making the most of humble ingredients, and positively enjoy turning a plain packet of semolina into a dish of melting, fragrant gnocchi, and this is what the book is about.

Although there is obviously no stopping convenience foods, turning to the shelves of the supermarket does not save you anything but time, since the pre-packed foods have been expensively prepared by other people, however cheaply they may have been bought in their original state, and are lavishly packaged and advertised. And if the people who enjoy feeding their families continue to carry their shopping baskets steadfastly past the supermarket door, in search of the odder cheap ingredients, then the shops will go on selling them, but if nobody asks for things like belly of pork and breast of lamb they will soon disappear for ever.

Eating cheaply does not mean buying inferior expensive ingredients, but good cheap ones. To cook them properly and keep the finished dish consistent with the idea of good eating, it is essential to have the right basic raw materials. This list of basics for a family store-cupboard includes necessities for the preparation of foods that need a helping hand to make them taste and look their best.

BASICS

Cheap **butter** for cooking

A large tin of **olive oil**

A large tin of **arachide oil** for deep frying. Keep separate bottles, one for fish and one for other things, and always strain the oil before it goes back in the bottle, or it will not stay fresh

Large chunk of **Parmesan cheese**

Tins and tins of Italian peeled **tomatoes**

Tubes or tins of **tomato purée**

Packets of **pasta** and **semolina**

Pounds of dried **haricot beans**, **kidney beans**, **flageolets** etc

Rice, long-grain for curry, Italian for risotto, round for puddings

Large bag of **dried mushrooms**r

Spices: coriander, cumin, turmeric, cardamom, chilli, paprika, allspice, mixed spice, cloves, cinnamon sticks, mace, nutmeg

Stock cubes chicken and beef.

Garlic

Herbs (do not keep them too long): bay leaves on a branch, rosemary, thyme, oregano, basil, marjoram, sage, tarragon. Keep parsley, chives and mint fresh in polythene bags in the refrigerator

Tins of **tuna fish**, **anchovies** in oil, **sardines**, **pimentoes**

Dijon **mustar**d, **mustard powder**

Sea salt, **peppercorns**

Olives: buy them loose and keep them fresh in a jar of oil

Plain flour and **baking powder**, instead of self-raising flour

Dried yeast or fresh yeast from the baker which keeps for up to a week in the refrigerator

Vanilla sugar: keep a pod of vanilla in a jar of caster sugar, and top it up as you need to

Wine vinegar

Dried fruit

(Don't keep anything for more than six months, or a year at most)

MEAT ROASTING TABLES

Quick Roast

For good quality meat: sear at Reg 8/230° for 15 minutes. Reduce to Reg 5/190° for the remainder of the cooking time.

Beef 15 minutes per lb plus 15 minutes for rare roasting. 20 minutes per lb plus 20 minutes for meat well done.

Lamb 25 minutes per lb plus 25 minutes.

Pork 35 minutes per lb plus 35 minutes.

Veal 30 minutes per lb plus 30 minutes.

Chicken 20 minutes per lb plus 20 minutes.

Turkey 8–10 lb bird 2–2½ hours

10–14 lb bird 2½–3 hours

14–20 lb bird 3½–4 hours

Slow Roast

Best for poor quality joints. It helps make them tender. Roast at Reg 3/160°.

Beef 40 minutes per lb plus 45 minutes.

Lamb 45 minutes per lb plus 45 minutes.

Pork Not suitable

Veal 50 minutes per lb plus 50 minutes

Chicken Over 4 lb, 25 minutes per lb plus 25 minutes.

Turkey 8–10 lb bird 3–3½ hours

10–14 lb bird 3½–4 hours

14–20 lb bird 4–5 hours

N.B. Bone is a good conductor of heat, so meat with the bone in does not need the extra minutes over. Stuffing on the other hand is a poor conductor, so add about fifteen minutes extra, depending on its thickness. Always judge the timing by the shape of the joint: a long thin piece will need less cooking than a compact thick one – use the chart as a general guide only.

METRIC CONVERSIONS

Weight

Imperial to metric (rounded up):

1 oz	30 g
2 oz	55 g
3 oz	85g
4 oz (¼ lb)	115 g
6 oz	170 g
8 oz (½ lb)	225 g
9 oz	255 g
10 oz	285 g
12 oz (¾ lb)	340 g
1 lb	450 g
1¼ lbs	565 g
1½ lbs	680 g
1¾ lbs	795 g
2 lbs	910 g

Liquid

Imperial to metric

¼ pint	140 ml
½ pint	285 ml
¾ pint	425 ml
1 pint	570 ml
1¼ pint	710 ml
1½ pint	850 ml
1¾ pint	1 litre
2 pints	1.15 litres

SOUPS

It is really easy to make home-made soup, and it always tastes much nicer than any out of a tin. The rustling of packets and clank of tin-openers may be a welcome sound but what appears in the soup-bowl a minute later has very little to do with the piping hot, delicately flavoured and beautifully coloured bowlful, with its handful of sizzling croutons or swirl of cream, that is your own vegetable soup. And the money saved by the manufacturers in buying vegetables by the ton is spent on packaging and massive advertising, so ready-made soups are not even particularly money-saving.

If you have a liquidiser, the making of soup is simply a question of cooking the right ingredients to the right degree of tenderness and then giving them a quick whizz, to puree them. If not, a Moulin-Legumes (or mouli), a small, inexpensive food mill for sieving soft fruit and cooked vegetables, is invaluable.

One of the vital ingredients for good soup is stock. Many cookery writers between the two wars decided stock should not be used in vegetable soups, because it overpowered the flavour of the vegetables and had a certain sameness to it that robbed the soup of its delicacy and freshness.

It is certainly true that if you use a strongly-flavoured or not altogether fresh stock you will end up with an awful failure. So use your own simple, freshly-made stock, obtained by putting chicken carcasses and bones in cold water, with a few carrots and an onion, plus a sprig of parsley, peppercorns and a bay leaf, and letting the liquid simmer and reduce incredibly slowly while you just go away and leave it. You can do the same with meaty beef or veal bones, freshly bought from the butcher; try to get marrow bones if you can, and remember to ask him to chop them up for you. Strain the stock, keep it in the refrigerator and use it within a day or two, then make a fresh lot. Or if you have a deep-freeze, you can keep a reserve of concentrated stock always available.

The day of the never-ending stock-pot to which a procession of old left-overs made its way daily is dead and gone; we don't like having that dreary, soggy-smelling

dishwater in our kitchens any more, and anyway there isn't room for it. For vegetable soup chicken stock really is the best, and if you haven't any it is perfectly feasible to use a stock-cube (Maggi tastes less of monosodium glutamate than others) but dilute it much more than it says in the directions or you will find that good old packet-soup flavour lurking in your own lovingly-made soup.

Chicken broth, as well as being the best stock, makes a marvellous basis for clear soups, and is a staple of many Italian kitchens, although one doesn't all that frequently get chicken to eat there. To it you can add pasta, poached eggs, marble-sized dumplings, finely sliced vegetables (which should be barely cooked when they are served), or a handful of rice and some egg-yolks beaten with fresh lemon juice. Do not, however, attempt a complicated mixture of different things or you may well end up with an indifferent sort of wet Russian salad.

The more filling soups, made with pasta and beans, meat and pearl barley, split peas and ham bones, should be served either as a meal on their own, with cheese and fruit afterwards, or before a very light, simple main dish such as an omelette or a salade Niçoise.

If you grow your own vegetables, you can use practically anything you have too much of to make a wonderful first course: French beans coming too fast to their best, lettuces that are getting ready to bolt, peas that have grown too fat, spinach you can't keep pace with, carrots, Jerusalem artichokes, reproachful turnips, beetroots or monstrous regiments of celery, disintegrating under the attack of vitamin-hungry slugs. If you don't have a vegetable garden you can still make use of gluts, and when the whole market is suddenly flooded with cheap tomatoes, that is the time to make tomato soup.

The beauty of a very humble soup, like carrot or turnip, or of any home-made soup in fact, is much more evident if you don't plonk it onto the table in a saucepan. A traditional china or earthenware soup tureen makes it look ten times more glorious. And having spent only a few pennies on the basic ingredients, the extra expense of a shilling on egg-yolks and cream can lift even quite a boring plain soup into luxuriousness, making it rich and velvety and lustrous, and a great compliment to the cook.

CONSOMMÉ

2-3 lbs beef or veal shin bones sawn up and with some meat on
2 pig's trotters split in four
3 onions
2 carrots
2 stalks celery
bouquet garni
6–7 peppercorns
salt
egg white
white wine, lemon juice or sherry

Consommé is gelatinous stock strong enough to form a jelly, which has been clarified to make it specklessly clear. It is useful for all sorts of dishes; they taste much more interesting with home-made rather than tinned consommé, and cost much less. Jellied eggs, a tarragon chicken in jelly, jellied cream cheese, all need a good stiffish consomme.

Pigs' or calves' feet contribute quite enough gelatine for a home-made consommé to stand up on its own, but if the weather is very hot, or you want it even stiffer than it is, you can add gelatine out of a packet at the very end. Put the bones and the pig's trotters in a large pan. Cover with 2 quarts cold water and bring slowly to the boil. Skim and add the vegetables cut in pieces, peppercorns and herbs. Simmer for 3–4 hours, covered; then add a little salt, simmer for another half-hour, strain and completely cool the stock so that the fat can be removed to the last speck, and you can see how strongly jellied your stock is. Return it to the stove and boil until it is reduced to the required amount to make it set. A glass of white wine or a dash of sherry at this stage is a good addition. Drop in the white of an egg beaten to a soft peak, and whisk it in. Boil it up until the froth rises in the pan, remove it from the heat and whisk again. Repeat the boiling and whisking twice more to make«sure the egg white is cooked. Put a cloth wrung out in hot water over a colander with a large wire strainer on top. Pour the stock through. The sediment will be caught in the egg white leaving the stock crystal clear. Add more sherry, lemon juice and salt to taste and heat. It will set to a beautiful jelly when cold.

CHICKEN BROTH WITH BUTTER DUMPLINGS

2 pints very good chicken broth
1½ oz butter
1 smail egg
1½ oz plain flour
1 oz self-raising flour
salt
chopped parsley
½ teaspoon grated lemon peel

Soften the butter and cream with the egg. Add the flour (both kinds), salt, parsley and lemon peel.

Add a little more plain flour if the mixture is too wet. Make little balls the size of a pea with the mixture. Drop these one by one into the simmering broth, cover and simmer ten minutes. The dumplings will swell nicely and be light as a feather.

These dumplings should be tiny and not at all filling.

For 4

EGG SOUP

½ pint very good clear stock (use chicken or beef cube if necessary, or use the consommé recipe, opposite)
1 slice crustless white bread
butter
1 egg
1 dessertspoon grated Parmesan if liked

Before you start, heat a soup-plate as much as you safely can; then, while the bouillon or stock is heating, fry the piece of bread golden on both sides in butter. Try to finish it just as the soup comes to boiling point. Put it quickly on the hot soup plate, break an egg on to the fried bread and pour the boiling liquid slowly on to the egg. Let it stand for three to four minutes before eating. The egg should be extremely lightly cooked by the combined heat of the plate, bread and soup. Sprinkle with cheese if liked.

For 1

STRACCIATELLA

2½ pints good clear chicken stock
2 eggs
2 tablespoons grated Parmesan (optional)
2 tablespoon semolina (optional)

Beat the eggs very well and add the cheese and semolina. Dilute with a cupful of cold stock. Heat the rest of the well-seasoned stock and as it approaches the boil gently pour in the egg mixture. Stir it with a fork in a clockwise direction rather fast.

Turn the heat really low and leave the soup slowly spinning for two to three minutes. Ideally the egg should form long, thin soft threads, but more often it looks like yellow snowflakes; never mind, it tastes the same.

A very good soup for convalescents and delicate stomachs.

For 4

KIDNEY SOUP

6 lambs' kidneys
½ oz butter
3 pints very good, but not salty, stock
2 oz flour
bouquet garni of thyme, parsley and bayleaf
1 blade mace
1 stick celery
6 peppercorns
salt to taste

Skin and halve the kidneys, removing the cores. Fry them in the butter in a saucepan until well browned, add the stock and bring gently to simmering point. Add the bouquet garni, mace, celery and peppercorns. Cover and simmer gently for one hour. Strain the liquid into a clean saucepan, remove the herbs, peppercorns and celery, and chop the kidneys finely.

Mix the flour in a large bowl with a little cold water, and add the reheated liquid just before it comes to the boil, stirring carefully to avoid lumps. Return it to the saucepan through a sieve, add the chopped kidneys and simmer, stirring, for five to ten minutes. Check seasoning, and serve with hot toast.

This is one of the best meat soups, thoroughly British and very rich.

For 5–6

SCOTCH BROTH

1 lb neck or breast of lamb
2 carrots
1 onion
2 leeks
½ small cabbage
1 stick celery
1 small turnip or slice of swede
2 tablespoons pearl barley
bunch parsley
salt and freshly ground pepper

Put the neck or breast of lamb in a large pan and cover with plenty of cold water. Bring to the boil and skim carefully. Throw in another cupful of cold water, bring to the boil and skim again. Simmer the meat while you clean all the vegetables and chop them small. Throw them and the pearl barley into the pan with the meat, add salt, pepper and half the parsley, and simmer gently, covered, for about two hours.

Remove the meat (if it is breast you can use it for epigrams, page 90) and keep it hot to eat with a caper sauce. Sprinkle a handful of freshly chopped parsley into the soup, taste for seasoning and serve.

For 4

ARTICHOKE SOUP

2 lbs Jerusalem artichokes
1 onion, peeled and sliced
parsley
1 pint stock
1 pint milk
nutmeg
salt, freshly ground pepper
butter
croutons or diced fried bacon

This is a very easily made and delicious soup. The only boring part is peeling the artichokes, and if they have only just come out of the ground you may not have to. But if they are already brown on the outside it is worth taking the trouble to do so as your soup will have an infinitely better colour and flavour.

Peel the artichokes and put them immediately into cold water acidulated with a dash of vinegar or lemon juice. Put the sliced onion and artichokes and a bunch of parsley tied with a thread into a large pan, cover with the stock and cook until tender, about 30 minutes. Take out the parsley. Sieve or liquidise finely, stir in the milk, reheat and add a large knob of butter, a grate of nutmeg and salt and pepper as needed. Serve with croutons or diced fried bacon.

For 4–5

CABBAGE SOUP

1 large onion
1 oz butter or lard
1 cabbage (about 1½ lbs, either white or Savoy)
½ lb soaked haricot beans or 2 cubed potatoes, or ½ lb haricots and 1 cubed potato
4 cloves garlic, peeled
3 pints fresh stock
large bunch parsley
hefty pinch thyme
salt and freshly ground pepper
large skinned tomatoes

Chop the onions and fry in butter or lard in a large, heavy saucepan. Add the chopped cabbage, soaked beans and/or potato cubes, garlic cloves, parsley, thyme and cold stock. Don't add salt yet. Bring it slowly to the boil; skim, and simmer gently, uncovered, for three hours. Add salt, pepper and the skinned, chopped tomatoes 30 minutes before the end. Serve with chopped parsley. It is really a glorious filling sort of stew, brown and very warming.

For 6

CARROT SOUP WITH OATMEAL

2 lbs carrots, scraped and sliced
2 stalks celery, chopped
2 onions, peeled and chopped
2 oz butter
2 teaspoons sugar
2 teaspoons salt
4 pints water or light chicken stock (can be made with a bouillon cube)
sprig of thyme
2 oz fine oatmeal
parsley, chopped
thin cream or top of the milk

Melt the butter in a large pan and add the celery, onions and carrots with sugar and salt. Sweat them for a few minutes, stirring, then pour on warm water or stock and add the sprig of thyme. Bring to a quiet simmer, cover and cook for 1½–2 hours. Sieve everything except the thyme into a clean pan. Mix the oatmeal with half a cup of milk or water to a smooth paste in a separate basin; add one or two ladles of the soup to the oatmeal, then stir the oatmeal mixture into the soup, taste for salt and simmer, stirring, for ten minutes. Stir in some cream or top of the milk. Add a sprinkling of parsley to each serving.

For 8

HOT CUCUMBER SOUP

1 small cucumber, peeled
1 medium-sized potato, peeled
4–5 spring onions
1½–2 pints good chicken stock
butter
salt and freshly ground pepper

Grate the potato and cucumber coarsely; strain off the liquid that forms and put the vegetables to sweat with the finely chopped onions in enough butter to cover the bottom of a medium saucepan. Heat the stock to simmering point and add to the vegetables. Simmer gently for 20–25 minutes. Check seasoning and serve with a knob of butter in each bowl.

Cucumber used to be eaten hot as often as cold; Eliza Acton recommends this highly, but lots of people have forgotten about it. It tastes quite different cooked, and is strangely interesting.

For 4

COLD CUCUMBER SOUP

1 cucumber
5 oz pot plain yoghurt
milk, straight out of the refrigerator
a couple of sprigs of fresh mint, chopped
salt, freshly ground pepper

In your liquidiser blend the peeled, chopped cucumber and yoghurt. Add enough milk to make up to one and a half pints. Chop the mint by hand and stir it in. Season and chill.

This is almost too simple if you have a liquidiser, but impossible if not. It is deliciously refreshing on a hot day.

For 4

LETTUCE SOUP

1 lettuce (keep the heart for sandwiches), or a few small lettuces
1 large onion
1 large potato
½ oz butter
1½ pints delicate chicken stock (or stock cube and water)
½ pint milk
salt and freshly ground black pepper
1 egg yolk (optional)

Wash the lettuce and break up the leaves; chop the onion and potato roughly. Melt the butter in a large pan and soften the lettuce and onion in it without browning. When they are soft add the potatoes and the boiling stock. Simmer uncovered for 20–30 minutes until the potatoes are cooked; sieve or liquidise for just a few seconds, moistening with milk. Add the rest of the milk and taste for seasoning. Heat through and serve with hot, well-fried croutons. An egg yolk, stirred in at the last moment, makes a much richer soup.

You can use sorrel to make this soup, or lettuce and sorrel together.

For 4

LEEK SOUP

1 lb leeks
onion
1½ oz butter
1½ oz flour
2 pints chicken or veal stock
salt and pepper
dash of cream or top of the milk or croutons or crisply fried bacon

Clean the leeks, leaving as much green as you can, and peel the onion. Chop both as finely as possible, which takes ages. Melt the vegetables in the butter in a large pan for about 15 minutes, stirring often, and without browning. Stir in the flour, allow it to thicken and then add the stock gradually. Season and simmer covered until the leeks are tender but still a pleasant green. Serve with croutons, or a spoonful of cream or little cubes of crisply fried bacon thrown sizzling into the soup bowls.

Very filling.

For 4–6

PASTA E FAGIOLI

6 oz haricot beans, previously soaked
3 medium potatoes, peeled and cubed
3 sticks celery, cut small
1 fennel root (if available) cut in strips
4 cloves garlic
salt and freshly ground pepper
4 oz short macaroni
parsley, chopped
2–3 tablespoons Parmesan, grated

Put the haricot beans in a large pan with two quarts of water, bring to the boil and cook gently for one hour, adding no salt. Then add the vegetables cut up small and the whole cloves of garlic. Add salt and pepper and simmer another 20–30 minutes until all the vegetables are tender, turn up the heat, and when the soup is gently boiling throw in the macaroni.

Chop a handful of parsley and throw it with the grated cheese into the soup as soon as the pasta is tender. Serve immediately. If the soup seems too thick, add a little more water. If it is too thin, you can stir in a couple of tablespoons of mashed potato, or if this is not available, ladle out some of the vegetables in the soup, puree them, and return them to the soup.

For 6–8

FRESH PEA SOUP

2 lbs fresh peas
1 bunch spring onions
½ chicken stock cube and 1 pint water or 1 pint fresh chicken stock
1 pint creamy milk
1 tablespoon cream
few chives, chopped
salt, pepper

Shell the peas and cook them with the chopped spring onions in the stock. When tender, sieve finely or put them through a liquidiser. Add the milk and heat through. Season. Serve with a tablespoon of cream and a sprinkling of chopped chives on each bowl. This is also good cold.

An absolutely simple and easy soupy delicate and a pretty pale green.

For 4

SPANISH SOUP

1 onion, 4 small leeks
1 small aubergine
3 small potatoes
½ pint stock
2–3 tomatoes
2 small red or gceen sweet peppers
4 oz French beans
2 cloves garlic
few sprigs parsley
pinch sweet paprika
olive oil, salt

Chop the peppers into one-inch squares, removing every seed. Simmer in oil for 30 minutes. Slice the onion across and quarter it. Cut the cleaned leeks into half-inch pieces. Cut the aubergine into cubes and sprinkle these with salt. Set them to drain.

Start cooking the onions and leeks in a pan with 1½ pints cold water. Cube the potatoes and add them after 15 minutes with ½ pint stock. Taste for seasoning. Skin and chop the tomatoes; add them to the soup after twenty minutes with the peppers, the rinsed aubergines and the beans broken in pieces. Cook until the beans are tender, then season again if necessary. Sprinkle chopped garlic and parsley and a large pinch of paprika into each plateful of soup.

This is a very adaptable soup. If you haven't got beans, leave them out; if you have courgettes, put them in; if you have marvellous fresh cabbage, put in a few good inner leaves, cut up. In Spain it is a real stand-by and they regard it as quick to make, which may explain why lunch is never ready until three o'clock.

For 2–3

TOMATO SOUP

1½ lbs tomatoes
½ oz butter, dash of oil
1 medium potato, peeled and chopped
1 medium onion, peeled and sliced
2 teaspoons sugar
1 teaspoon salt
1½ pints water
sprig of parsley
bayleaf, or, if available, some basil
1 tablespoon tomato puree (optional)

Chop the tomatoes roughly but leave the skins on. Melt the butter in a saucepan with the oil and cook the potato and onion until they start to soften.

They tend to stick so stir them with a wooden spoon. Add the tomatoes and let them soften. Add salt, sugar, pepper, herbs and water. Simmer uncovered until the potatoes are cooked. Remove the bayleaf, and sieve, mouli or liquidise everything else. Reheat just before serving, correct seasoning. Add tomato puree if it is too pale, which will depend a lot on the tomatoes you use. Anyway it won't be a fierce orange like tinned tomato soup but a much prettier soft orangey red. Stir a little cream into each plate as you serve it.

This soup is much more delicate than it sounds.

For 6

TWO OF EVERYTHING SOUP

2 medium-sized leeks
2 medium-sized carrots
2 medium-sized potatoes
1½–2 pints boiling water
salt
milk, if necessary
knob of butter
croutons for garnish, if liked

Into a large saucepan put the potatoes and carrots cleaned and cut into inch-square pieces, and the leeks, including all the good green parts, cut in inch-long slices. Pour on enough boiling water to cover the vegetables by half an inch. Add ½ teaspoon salt. Cover the pan and simmer the soup for three-quarters to one hour, or up to two hours or more if you want to go out, but it must cook very gently.

Put the soup through the liquidiser, return it to the cleaned pan, bring it back to the boil and simmer it gently for five minutes. If it is too thick add a little milk; if too thin, cook a little longer. It should be the consistency of thin cream. Taste for salt, add a knob of butter and serve plain or garnished with small.croutons of fried bread.

For 4

LEMON SPINACH SOUP

1 small onion or shallot
1 lb spinach
1½ pints stock
½ lemon
2 egg yolks
salt
handful rice (optional)

Chop the onion finely and the spinach coarsely. Simmer in the stock, uncovered, for about 20 minutes until tender. Sieve or liquidize. Pour the soup back into the pan. Beat the egg yolks in a bowl and add two tablespoons of the hot (not boiling or even simmering) soup. Add this to the soup in the pan with the juice of half a lemon. Season and heat very, very gently but don't simmer or it will curdle. Serve very hot.

No garnish is necessary.

If you want a more filling soup you can add a handful of rice, boiled and still hot, with the egg and lemon juice.

For 4

WATERCRESS SOUP

2 bunches watercress
2–3 large potatoes
1 onion
1½ pints stock (or stock cube and water)
1 pint milk
salt and freshly ground pepper
knob of butter

Put the potatoes and onion, peeled and roughly chopped, into a large pan. Add cold stock, bring to the boil and simmer for 15-20 minutes; now throw in the washed watercress, stalks and all, and cook until it is tender but still a good green. Sieve all this, helping it through the mouli by moistening with the milk. If you want a green-flecked soup, use a coarse disc for your mouli; if a uniform green, use a finer disc. You can do either with a liquidiser by adjusting the timing. Now add enough milk to make the soup a good consistency. Return the soup to the stove, season and heat through. Serve with a nut of butter and a sprig of watercress in each plate.

If you sweat the watercress and onion in butter before adding the potato and stock, you make a slightly richer soup. The watercress looks best very coarsely chopped to make large green flecks.

For 6

TURNIP SOUP

5 medium turnips, peeled and coarsely chopped
2 tablespoons butter
1 large onion, finely chopped
2–3 pints boiling water
4–5 slices bread
2 egg yolks
½ pint thin cream or top of the milk
salt, freshly ground pepper

Cook the turnips and onion in butter, in a large pan, until they start to soften, but not to brown. Add boiling water and seasoning and crumble in the bread, crusts removed. Simmer gently until the vegetables are tender (25–30 minutes). Sieve or liquidise. Beat the egg yolks with the cream and add to the re-heated soup, away from the heat. Stir over a low heat until smooth and creamy, without boiling or even simmering, and serve with a nut of butter in each bowl.

For 4–6

VICHYSSOISE

1 !b leeks
2–3 medium potatoes
1 onion
parsley
1 pint chicken stock
1 pint creamy milk
salt and white pepper
chives
thin cream (optional)

Clean and chop the leeks, peel and slice the potatoes and onion. Put the vegetables in a pan with the parsley tied in a bundle, and cover with the stock. Simmer until all the vegetables are tender. Remove the parsley, then sieve the vegetables, helping them through the sieve by moistening with milk. Add the rest of the milk, just enough to make a thinnish creamy soup, season with salt and a little freshly ground white pepper, and chill. Serve cold with chopped chives and a thread of cream ityou have it. This tastes very good hot if the weather suddenly turns cold.

A well-known mid-Atlantic soup.

For 4

CHICK PEA SOUP

6–8 oz chick peas
olive oil
1 clove garlic, chopped
1 onion, peeled and sliced
1 green pepper, de-seeded and chopped
3 anchovy fillets, chopped
3 tomatoes, skinned and chopped
pinch rosemary
4 oz short macaroni
salt

Soak chick peas overnight, or all day. Put in a large pan, cover with plain cold water and bring slowly to the boil. Simmer gently, adding more boiling water if necessary, for two to three hours until tender. Add no salt yet. Cover the bottom of a sauté pan with olive oil and sauté the onions, garlic, peppers and anchovies over a moderate heat until tender. Add the tomatoes and a pinch of chopped rosemary. Simmer five or ten minutes more, then add this mixture to the chick peas and their liquid. Season with salt at this point and bring to the boil. Add the macaroni and cook the soup until the macaroni is tender. It should taste as though it is made with a really good beef-broth – the anchovies make this contribution to the soup.

For 4

DUTCH PEA SOUP

1 lb dried peas (split green ones)
1 knuckle green bacon, soaked overnight
1 fresh pig's trotter (if salt, soak overnight)
2 onions, peeled and chopped
2 leeks, cleaned and cut up
3 sticks celery
4–5 frankfurters
butter for frying

Soak the peas for two to four hours. Take a large saucepan and put in the drained peas; cover with six pints water, and simmer, covered, without salt for one or two hours. Add the bacon and pig's trotter and simmer two hours more. In a separate pan soften the fresh vegetable in butter while you sieve or liquidise the pea soup, having first removed the meat to a plate. Add the softened vegetables to the pureed pea soup and cook on for an hour more, over a very low heat. Stir from time to time to prevent it from catching. Leave, covered, overnight. Next day chop the meat from the knuckle into small pieces, and add it with the sliced frankfurters to the soup, which should have set solid. Heat through, taste for seasoning, and if the pea-starch, which expands, has made it too thick, add a little water. You can adjust the amount of bacon and sausages to the number of people and their appetites. The pig's foot is thrown out, but it does a lot for the texture of the soup and adds nourishment.

This soup is very filling and can be eaten as a meal on its own. It is best if made the day before.

For 6–8

LENTIL SOUP

½ lb green lentils
2 pints water or beef stock
1 onion
1 stick celery
4 cloves garlic
salt and freshly ground pepper
butter
1–2 potatoes, cubed

Soak the lentils overnight. Bring them slowly to the boil in the water or stock, and skim. In a separate pan soften the finely chopped onion, garlic and sliced celery in a little butter. Add the lentils in their boiling stock and the potato cubes. Season with salt and pepper. Simmer gently until the lentils are cooked, about one hour.

The soup should be a rich dark brown and is very filling.

For 4

COCKLE CHOWDER

2 quarts cockles, well washed and scrubbed
4 rashers bacon, cut small
1oz butter
1 Spanish onion, chopped
2–3 parboiled floury potatoes, cut into cubes
½ pint milk (or up to 1 pint)
handful chopped parsley
freshly ground pepper

Bring an inch of water to the boil in a large pan with a lid. Throw in the cockles, put on the lid and leave over a high flame. Shake the pan from time to time, or stir the cockles once or twice with a wooden spoon; after four to five minutes all the shells should be open and the cockles slightly cooked.

Remove all the shells, put the cockles aside and strain the liquid through a cloth. In another pan melt one ounce of butter, let the pieces of bacon sizzle in it, add the onion and cook gently until it is transparent. Add the potatoes, £ pint of the strained cockle liquid, and the milk. Let this simmer very gently until the potatoes are soft but not a total mush. Add the shelled cockles, pepper and parsley; heat thoroughly but gently, and test for saltiness (it should not need any extra salt as the cockle liquid is salty, and so is the bacon).

Serve with thick, hard ships' biscuits. Lovers of *Moby Dick* might break their biscuits into the soup

An English seaside version of clam chowder.

For 4

ITALIAN COCKLE SOUP

2 quarts cockles, fresh and very well washed
½ pint water
½ pint olive oil
1 clove garlic, chopped fine
small handful parsley, chopped fine
2–3 anchovy fillets, chopped
1 tablespoon tomato purée diluted in ¼ pint water,or ½ pint fresh tomato sauce
small glass white wine
oregano
4 slices bread, fried crisp in olive oil at the last minute

Open the cockles by boiling fast, covered, in a large pan with ¾ pint water. Shake the pan a couple of times and remove the cockles when they have all opened. Strain the liquid scrupulously through a damp cloth, while you prepare the rest of the soup. In another large pan heat the oil, add garlic, parsley, anchovies and wine. Let it simmer five minutes, add the tomato puree, diluted, or tomato sauce, and simmer gently four or five minutes more.

Add the cockles, most of their shells removed as they clutter up the plate rather, the oregano and the strained liquid, and simmer three to four minutes more while you put one slice of hot, golden, fried bread in each soup plate. Pour the soup, shells and all, over the fried bread and serve straight away. You probably will not need salt as the cockles exude sea water.

This soup has a good pungent Mediterranean flavour. You can make it very well with mussels if cockles are not available.

For 4

MOULES MARINIERES

1 or 2 quarts mussels, depending on how greedy you are
2oz butter
1 medium onion, finely chopped
1 clove garlic (if liked)
small glass white wine
handful of fresh parsley, finely chopped
freshly ground pepper

Scrape, scrub and thoroughly clean the mussels under running cold water. Throw away any which float, or are open or damaged. Melt the butter and fry the onion gently in a capacious saucepan with a well-fitting lid; add garlic as and if you like. When the onion is transparent, after about 15 minutes, grind in some pepper and pour in a small glass of white wine; let it bubble a minute. Now add the mussels and slarn on the lid, turning up the heat as high as it will go. Shake the pan once or twice, and after about four or five minutes, look. It is ready if all the shells are wide open. Ladle the mussels, as they are, into a hot china tureen. Strain the now considerable amount of liquid over them carefully, because in spite of your cleaning it may still be gritty. Sprinkle chopped green parsley over the shiny black-blue shells and serve, providing another dish for empty shells. It should need no salt if the mussels are fresh and have recently been living in the sea.

If you find your own mussels do make sure they aren't living near a drain. Soak them for a couple of hours in fresh water, or their liquid will be much too salty to drink in the soup.

This is very simple.

For 2

FISH SOUP (VELOUTÉ D'EPERLANS)

1 pint milk, infused with a sliced onion and a bayleaf
1 slice home-made type white bread
1oz butter
1 medium onion, finely chopped
1 lb skinned fillets lemon sole, plaice or whiting
4 oz smelts
½ pint thin Bechamel sauce (page 137)
pinch cayenne pepper
salt
chives

Cut the crusts off the bread and pour on a little of the strained hot milk. Pound to a paste (panada), gradually adding the rest of the milk. Add the chopped onion, cayenne and salt. Poach the fish fillets in this for 30 minutes. Don't worry if it looks odd at this stage. Meanwhile make the Bechamel and stew the cleaned smelts in 1 oz butter without browning them. Sieve the panada mixture, or pass through the mouli with the flesh from the smelts and the butter in which they were cooked. Help the mixture through with extra milk if it gets too dry. Add the sieved mixture to the Bechamel sauce and mix in thoroughly. Season and heat through. If the soup is too thick, add extra milk. Serve with chopped chives on top.

The smelts have a very strong flavour; use very few or they will be overpowering.

For 4

SMOKED HADDOCK SOUP

1 medium smoked haddock (12 oz)
water
1 onion, chopped and peeled
1 pint milk
few tablespoons mashed potato
4 oz butter
salt and freshly ground pepper
parsley

Skin the haddock, and set the skin aside. Put the haddock in a shallow pan and pour on enough boiling water to cover. Bring slowly to the boil, then add the chopped onion. When tender remove it from the pan, take the flesh off the bones and flake it. Put the bones and skin back in the pan and simmer, covered, for one hour. When the stock is thoroughly flavoured, strain it, bring it to the boil again, and add the milk, brought to the boil in a separate pan, and the flaked fish. Slowly add enough mashed potato to give the soup a creamy consistency. At the last moment taste for salt and pepper and stir in the butter. Serve sprinkled with chopped parsley, or put another lump of butter in each bowl.

For 4

EGGS AND CHEESE

It is a long time since everybody living in the country had a coop of laying hens in the orchard, and foxes and broodiness were genuine threats to the family egg supply. Eggs, packed in their own beautiful fragile shells, are abundant, and farms with a quarter of a million chickens apiece keep the poor birds laying night and day. Luckily, although one may not approve of chickens being treated as egg-laying units, the massive production methods and subsidies do mean that eggs stay comparatively cheap, and therefore it is worth being lavish with them; they are such an incredibly un wasteful way of handing out first-class protein, and after all, a really perfect souffle is just as much of a treat as a fresh salmon trout or a fillet of beef, and is very much easier to make than people suppose.

It is probably worth buying large eggs for eating and small eggs to use in cooking, for cakes, sauces, and for brushing the tops of pies and so on. Otherwise this can be wasteful, though both yolks and white can be kept in the refrigerator, covered with foil. Eggs in their shells do not have to be kept in the refrigerator. They are so beautiful and they get eaten up so quickly, it is surely more sense to keep them somewhere they can offer the cook a bit of inspiration; anyway, lots of sauces can't easily be made with a chilled egg.

One of the greatest companions for eggs is cheese. We are only concerned here with cheese for cooking, and the recipes use a tremendous amount of Parmesan and Swiss Emmenthal, or Gruyere, which is similar but with smaller and less frequent holes. These are not the cheapest cheeses there are by any means, but they are invaluable in the kitchen because they cook so well, and keep for weeks, scarcely suffering at all; however dry they get they can still be used for grating. Keep them wrapped in greaseproof paper in the larder or refrigerator. Many Italian provision shops and delicatessens sell Parmesan, but if the price really staggers you, there are cheaper, slightly stronger, versions of it: Pecorino Romano, which is called Vacchino Romano when made with cow's milk, and Caprino Romano when made with goat's milk, and Sardo which is the same cheese but made in Sardinia. It really is an extravagance to buy ready-grated

Parmesan in little pots; not only does it cost more, but it tastes terrible. If you cannot go often to an Italian supplier, invest in a really large lump of one of the grating cheeses: it is worth the pain of momentary extravagance.

Good cooking cheeses, which can always be substituted for the imported ones if necessary, are Cheddar and Cheshire (or Chester as the French call it). Fresh Mozzarella, which is referred to in one or two recipes, is another Italian cheese, soft and round and white, which traditionally was made with buffaloes' milk, but now probably only of cows' milk, and which should be stored in a bowl of cold water in the refrigerator. It is dull on its own, but wonderful with a salad or cooked, when it becomes rich and succulent. If it is not available, Bel Paese is a fairly good substitute.

SCRAMBLED EGG

It was Boulestin who raised scrambled egg from a humble breakfast dish to the sort of food you could offer your friends and guests. He was right: there is nothing more delicious than well scrambled egg and there are lots of variations on the plain creamy golden sort that one eats when alone in the house.

How to cook scrambled egg, if you haven't already got a perfect method. Melt a large lump of butter in a saucepan, add as many lightly beaten eggs as you need, seasoned with salt and pepper, and stir continuously with a wooden spoon over a medium to low heat until you have a pan of creamy eggs. Take it off the heat just before you think it is set as it goes on cooking, by its own heat and that of the pan, for a few seconds.

VARIATIONS ON SCRAMBLED EGG

Make scrambled egg as usual and before it sets add one of the following:

1. cold cooked salmon, flake
2. cold cooked smoked haddock, flaked
3. grated cheese or cheese cut in little squares

4. mussels, cockles or fresh shrimps, cooked and shelled

5. anchovies previously soaked in milk and drained

6. chopped tarragon or chives or a combination of parsley, chives and chervil

7. skinned chopped tomato, first grilled whole

8. chopped ham or tongue

or before adding to the scrambled egg, cook one of the following in butter:

1. sliced button mushrooms

2. chopped chicken livers

3. cubes of bacon

4. cubes of cooked potato

5. skinned diced lambs'kidneys

6. chopped spring onions

or serve plain scrambled egg

1. in an open, buttered and seasoned baked potato

2. on a bed of spinach

or make a Pipérade

PIPÉRADE

2 medium onions
2 cloves garlic
3 tablespoons oil
2 red peppers
4 tomatoes, skinned
4 eggs
salt and freshly ground pepper

Melt the sliced onions in the oil in a heavy pan, add the crushed cloves of garlic and cook gently, without browning, for 15 minutes. Meanwhile slice up the peppers, removing all the seeds, add them to the onions, and cook on without browning until the peppers are tender. Chop the tomatoes and add them to the stew. Add a little salt and simmer on for about 25 minutes until the mixture is moist but not wet. Now beat the eggs lightly in a bowl, season with salt and pepper and stir them into the vegetables as you would for scrambled eggs. When the eggs begin to thicken, it is cooked.

Serve it in a plain earthenware dish with triangles of fried bread, or have mounds of fresh bread and butter on the table.

This was originally a dish eaten by Basque sailors; it is both rich and simple.

For 4

TO MAKE BAKED EGGS

First method – straight forward and easy:

Heat the oven to Reg 4/180°. Butter the cocottes and season with salt and freshly ground pepper before you put the eggs in. Put a baking tin half full of water to warm up on top of the cooker.

Gently lower the cocottes with their eggs into the hot water and go on gently heating until the eggs look cloudy at the bottom. Then put the whole thing in the centre of the oven for 15–20 minutes, while you gently heat some seasoned cream in a pan. Look to see if the eggs are set, and if so take them out of the oven and put them on to plates before pouring the hot cream on them. .

Second method – quicker but trickier:

Heat the oven to Reg 4/180°. Butter the cocottes and break an egg into each. Pour on enough cream to cover each egg completely. Season with salt and freshly ground pepper, and place in the oven. After 15 minutes keep looking at the eggs and shaking them to see if they are cooked. When the white under the cream just won't shiver, but before it is solid, they are cooked.

One or two per person.

TO POACH AN EGG

Shallow pan of boiling salted water with a tablespoon of vinegar or lemon juice in it
Eggs (very fresh)

First method

When two inches of water is boiling in the pan, turn it down to a perceptible simmer and break an egg, sliding it into a nice still part of the pan. With a spoon keep the white together. Let it simmer until completely opaque. Lift out carefully with a slotted spoon.

Second method

When the water, about three inches deep, is boiling, whirl it round gently with a spoon or fork, and break the egg into the water. When the egg hits the water the strands of egg white will neatly spin round the yolk with the action of the water. It will sink to the bottom of the pan but rise to the surface as it cooks. Lift it out with a slotted spoon after three to four minutes. Drain well.

To cook more than one egg

Use a larger pan, break them all into one bowl and slip the whole lot into the water at once. Lift out gently one at a time, or two by two and separate them when you have them on a plate or dish. Drain well.

OEUFS MOLLETS AUX FINES HERBES

1 (or 2) egg(s) for each person
4 oz butter per egg
3 or 4 twigs tarragon
3 or 4 sprigs parsley or, better still, chervil
bunch of chives
salt and freshly ground pepper

Bring a pan of water to a steady boil, put in the eggs, which should be at room temperature, not straight out of the fridge, and boil them for exactly five and a half minutes, six for large eggs. Remove and hold under the cold tap until they are cool enough to handle. Tap the shell of each egg carefully all over. Peel with great concentration or large chunks of the white will come zipping out and the egg will sag and crack. When the eggs are shelled they should be soft but not so soft that they break open. Keep them warm in a bowl of warm water.

Melt the butter but don't let it sizzle or start to brown, Strip the tarragon leaves off the stalks and chop the herbs together finely. Stir them into the butter, add a little salt and pepper and pour it over the drained eggs. Serve hot. They won't be absolutely scalding hot, they aren't meant to be.

For 2–4

OEUFS EN GELÉE

4 eggs
½ pint jellied home made consommé (page 12) or one tin consommé
2 tablespoons sherry, if there is none in the consommé
2 slices smoked ham
tarragon or flat parsley

Stir the sherry into the melted consommé. In a separate pan poach the eggs carefully. The yolks should still be runny, otherwise the results will be very disappointing. When they are cooked add half a pint of cold water to the pan to prevent them cooking any more, unless you are ready to use them immediately, in which case lift them carefully out of the water and drain them a little. Trim off the rough outside edges. Lay half a slice of ham, folded up, in the bottom of each of four cocottes. Lay a trimmed egg carefully on to each. Lay the tarragon leaves or parsley in a pattern on top of each egg and pour in enough consomme to come just over the top of each egg. Let them set in a cool place. Some people put pate in the bottom instead of ham but this can be rather sickly.

Make these the day before you want to eat them.

For 4

OEUFS BENEDICTINE

4 eggs, poached
For Hollandaise (page 138)
2 extra yolks
squeeze lemon juice
4 oz butter
salt and pepper
4 large tablespoons creamed smoked haddock (page 64)
4 rounds fried bread

Spread a layer of haddock puree on each piece of fried bread, put a poached egg on top and pour the Hollandaise sauce over. Serve straight away. This was originally made with salt cod, never with ham (though that can be nice too), as it was a Lenten dish.

For 4

TO MAKE AN OMELETTE

2 or 3 eggs
salt and pepper
butter

Beat the eggs lightly in a bowl with a little salt and pepper. You can add a tablespoon of water but it is not essential to a good omelette. Melt a large hazelnut of butter in a steel omelette pan used only for its proper purpose. Swirl the butter round to coat the bottom and sides of the pan, and when it starts to brown pour in the eggs at once. Keep a wooden fork or spoon to make omelettes, as a metal one would spoil the surface of the pan. Over a medium heat stir the centre of the omelette briefly. Then, tipping the pan this way and that, lift the setting sides of the omelette to let the uncooked egg on top get to the heat. When there is no more uncooked egg give the pan a short brisk jerk to loosen the omelette, tip to start it rolling over, and help it with your fork; roll it out of the pan on to the middle of a warm plate. It should be plump and juicy and not very brown.

For 1

OMELETTE ARNOLD BENNETT

1 smoked haddock on the bone (about 1 lb)
½ pint milk
½ pint water
3 oz butter
1½ oz flour
2 oz Parmesan, Emmenthal or Cheddar cheese, grated
salt and freshly ground pepper
8 eggs

Trim tail and collar bones from the haddock and poach gently in half a pint each of milk and water, until the bones come away easily. Make a thick Bechamel sauce with the flour, half the butter and the cheese, using some of the liquid in which

the fish has cooked. There should be About half a pint of thickish sauce. Bone the fish and put the flaked pieces into the sauce, reserving about three tablespoons of sauce. Season with pepper and add salt if necessary. Keep it warm while you beat the eggs lightly with a little salt and pepper. Fold the fish mixture into the eggs.

Preheat the grill and a serving dish. Heat the remaining butter in a thick heavy frying pan, tipping it from side to side until it is just starting to brown. Gently pour in the mixture, using the reserved sauce to make a pattern on the top of the omelette, rather like a hot cross bun. Cook gently, allowing the uncooked egg to reach the heat by lifting the omelette carefully and tipping the pan.

When it is set underneath, but still undercooked on top, sprinkle with more cheese and put under a hot grill until the top is just a little brown here and there. Slide it on to a large heated dish, not too hot or the omelette will go on cooking, and serve at once, cut in slices like a cake. The top and bottom should be firmly set and the inside still juicy and slightly runny.

For 4 (main course), or 8 (first course)

OMELETTE IN AN OVERCOAT

8 eggs
½ lb mushrooms
3 oz butter
½ pint single cream
salt and freshly ground black pepper
1 oz flour
½ pint milk
1 oz Parmesan, freshly grated
2 oz Gruyere, freshly grated

Slice the mushrooms and cook them in two ounces of the butter. Add the cream, salt and plenty of freshly ground pepper and reduce until the mixture thickens. Keep the mushrooms warm while you make a cheese sauce with the remaining butter, flour, milk, salt, pepper and cheese; a dribble of cream kept from the quarter pint could well go into this sauce, it makes it brown so beautifully. With the eight eggs, beaten lightly and seasoned, make a very large omelette into which you put the creamy mushroom filling.

Fold the omelette on to a hot (but not very hot) serving plate and pour the cheese sauce all over it. Put the omelette under a hot grill for a minute or two and watch it. When it is a beautiful brown serve it immediately with a green salad.

For 4

ONION AND POTATO OMELETTE

6 eggs
salt and pepper
4 potatoes
1 medium onion
butter and oil, for frying

Peel and boil the potatoes. Chop the onion finely and soften in very little oil and butter without browning. Add the cubed cooked potatoes and heat them thoroughly, even brown them a bit. Beat the eggs briefly with salt and pepper, make the omelette as usual and add the potato and onion mixture, spreading it all over, half-way through the cooking. Cook on as usual and serve with a green salad.

This is a sort of tortilla *but it requires fewer potatoes and more eggs, and is cooked less fiercely than the real thing.*

For 4

SOUFFLE CHEESE OMELETTE

8 eggs
1oz flour
1oz butter
½ pint milk
salt and freshly ground pepper
2oz Emmenthal cheese, grated
2oz Parmesan cheese, grated
top of the milk
butter for cooking the omelette

Make a thickish cheese sauce with the butter, flour, milk and grated cheese; add a little top of the milk and seasoning and beat the sauce well until it is glossy.

Separate the egg yolks from the whites; beat the whites until they are fluffy. Preheat the grill and a serving dish. Beat the yolks with a little salt and pepper. Heat a tablespoon of butter in a large frying pan, swirling it over the sides and bottom to prevent the omelette from sticking. Rapidly fold the whites into the yolks and when the butter starts to brown slip the mixture into the pan. Let it cook over a moderate heat without stirring until set and golden brown underneath. Then put the pan under the grill for a minute or two.

Slide the omelette on to the hot dish, folding it in half. Pour the sauce over it and put it back under the grill to brown quickly. Serve straight away. The omelette should be fluffy inside and the sauce creamy and rich. Eat with a green salad.

This is a very good main course; it isn't heavy but it is filling.

For 4

CHEESE SOUFFLE

1 ½ oz butter
1oz flour
½ pint milk
3 oz cheese, grated
3 egg yolks and 4 whites
salt and cayenne pepper

Preheat the oven to Reg 7/220°. Prepare a souffle dish 5–6 inches in diameter, by buttering liberally and then coating the inside with flour, shaking out any excess.

Make a Bechamel (see page 137) then add the cheese, stirring all the time. Season with salt and cayenne pepper, remove from the heat and beat in the egg yolks one at a time. Take this mixture off the heat while you beat the egg whites to a firm snow. Add one tablespoon of whites to the sauce and stir it in, then fold in the remaining egg whites, add more salt and cayenne pepper if necessary, and turn lightly into the souffle dish. Put in the oven, turn down the heat to Reg 6/200° and bake 20–25 minutes. Serve straight away while it is brown and puffy and light. Souffles are definitely better a bit sloppy inside than dry and overcooked. They are nowhere near as sensitive as people think and it is really quite difficult to make a failure – as long as people are ready and waiting when the souffle is just right. There is only one answer and that is to have everyone at the table, forks in hand.

For 4

LITTLE TOMATO SOUFFLES

6 really large tomatoes
1oz flour
1oz butter
2 tablespoons cream
1 tablespoon Parmesan, grated
4 eggs plus one white
salt, freshly ground pepper

Preheat the oven to Reg 7/220°. Cut the tomatoes in half and scoop out the insides. Simmer the juice and pulp for a few minutes in a small pan. Sieve and use this purée, seasoned with a little salt and pepper, to make a stiffish sauce with the butter, flour, cream and grated Parmesan. When the sauce has cooled a little, stir in four egg yolks, one at a time, beating each one in well. Beat the five egg whites to a soft light foam. Beat two tablespoons of this into the tomato mixture, and then add the rest, folding it in carefully. Dry the insides of the tomato halves, season and fill them to the top with the mixture. Put into the hot oven. After five minutes turn the heat down to Reg 6/200° and cook for 15–20 minutes until light brown on top. .

For 6

SMOKED HADDOCK SOUFFLE

1 small smoked haddock on the bone – approx. ¾ lb
½ pint milk
½ pint water
knob of butter
1½ oz flour
2 oz butter
4 eggs plus 1 egg white
1 oz Parmesan, freshly grated
1 oz Gruyere, freshly grated
salt and freshly ground pepper

Preheat oven to Reg 6/200°. Cook the haddock in the milk and water with a knob of butter for ten minutes. Do not let it catch on the bottom of the pan; it is a good idea to cook it skin side up. When it is cooked, strain off the liquid and keep half a pint. Flake the haddock, removing the skin and bones, and chop finely with a knife or flake very small. Make a thick sauce with the flour, butter and half a pint of the haddock liquid, and beat in the grated cheese, keeping a tablespoon or so of Parmesan on one side. Add the haddock, and remove from the heat. Beat in the egg yolks one by one and season the sauce with salt if necessary, and plenty of pepper. Butter a three pint souffle dish and dust the inside with grated cheese. If you use a large dish you don't have to fiddle with paper collars etc.

Beat the egg whites stiffly. Stir a quarter into the haddock mixture, fold in the rest with a palette knife, turn into the souffle dish, levelling out the top, and put straight into the oven.Turn the heat down to Reg 5/160° and bake 25–30 minutes until very brown and puffy. Eat it the instant it is out of the oven, with a green salad. It makes a perfect lunch.

Smoked haddock combines exceptionally well with eggs, and this is one of the best souffles of all.

For 3–4

FISHERMAN'S TOAST

4 slices slightly stale white bread, crusts removed
2 eggs, beaten with salt
milk
dripping, butter or bacon fat

Soak the slices of bread in milk, then dip them in the beaten egg. Melt the fat in a large frying-pan and fry the bread slices until golden both sides. Very good for breakfast or supper. A sweet version uses sugar instead of salt; fry in butter or oil and serve sprinkled with sugar, when it is known as pain perdu.

Two eggs do for four people.

For 4 children

EGG CROQUETTES

1½ oz butter
1½ oz flour
½ pint milk, previously infused with a sliced onion, 6 peppercorns and a bayleaf
4 hard-boiled eggs
flour
1 beaten egg
dried breadcrumbs
salt, freshly ground pepper, and a pinch of nutmeg
oil for deep frying
bacon (optional)

Make a stiff Bechamel with the butter, flour and flavoured milk (see page 137). Peel the hard-boiled eggs and sieve the yolks into the sauce. Add the whites, coarsely chopped, season well and add a good pinch of nutmeg. Run a china plate under the cold tap for a few seconds, then spread the mixture on it and leave covered in a cool place for several hours. It should set firmly enough to roll into small cork shapes about 2 ins. long. Roll these in flour, dip in beaten egg and then coat with breadcrumbs. Deep fry in oil, drain on kitchen paper, and serve very hot either on their own or with tomato sauce.

You can put chopped bacon, lightly fried, into the mixture with the chopped, hard-boiled egg.

These ideally should be made a day ahead as the mixture becomes easier to handle after standing several hours.

For 4

EGGS IN A NEST

1½ lbs potatoes
milk, nutmeg, butter, salt, freshly ground pepper – for mashed potatoes
cheese, grated
8 eggs
butter

Peel and cut up the potatoes. Boil them until tender in salted water. Sieve or mash, using plenty of hot milk and butter. When light and fluffy, season with salt, pepper and a pinch of nutmeg and add two tablespoons of grated cheese. Butter a shallow oven dish of glass or china, put in the mashed potatoes and make eight depressions with the back of a spoon. Gently break an egg into each hollow and sprinkle with a little more grated cheese and some small pieces of butter. Season with a little salt and pepper. Bake at Reg 4/180°, until the eggs are set (10–20 minutes). Serve at once. The yolks should be runny and the whites firm.

Very good for children's lunch and for using up mashed potatoes.

For 4

EGGS IN BAKED POTATOES

6 eggs
6 large, perfect potatoes
butter
single cream
salt and freshly ground pepper
freshly grated Parmesan cheese

Bake the potatoes in the oven, Reg 2½/155°, for 2 hours, cool a little and through a hole in the top scoop out enough of the insides to make room for an egg. Put in a knob of butter, salt and pepper. Break an egg into each, add a little cream and Parmesan and bake in a hot oven, Reg 6/180°, for about 15 minutes or until the eggs are set.

Very good for children's lunch.

For 6

EGGS IN THEIR DISH

2 eggs
1 small onion, chopped
1 tomato, peeled and chopped
salt and freshly ground pepper
oil, butter or bacon fat for frying
additional if liked
1 or 2 rashers of bacon, cut small, or
1 sliced cooked potato, or
pieces of salami, or
pieces of red or green pepper

Using a very small frying pan, fry the onion gently in a teaspoon of fat or oil, until it is transparent but not coloured. (Put any bacon, potato, pepper or salami in with the onion.) Peel and chop the tomato. Add it to the onion, season with salt and pepper. Wait until the tomato is beginning to soften but not until it disintegrates. Gently break one or two eggs onto the bed of onion etc. Cook gently. When the bottom is set dot the top with a little butter and finish under a medium grill. The eggs are half poached, half fried and you eat them straight from the dish.

A very quick lunch if you are by yourself

For 1

CROQUE MONSIEUR

2 slices bread
1 slice ham, with not too much fat
1 thin slice Gruyere
½ oz butter
½ tablespoon oil

Cut the crusts off the bread and thinly butter one side of each slice. Make a sandwich with the slice of ham and slice of Gruyere and press firmly shut.

Heat a frying pan with the butter and a dash of oil, and when hot fry the sandwich. Both sides (turn carefully) should be pale

gold and the cheese starting to melt; eat at once. It is the French version of Mozzarella in Carrozza (below).

For 1

MOZZARELLA IN CARROZZA

2 eggs
8 slices home-made type white bread (preferably slightly stale)
2 Mozzarella cheeses
salt and pepper
olive oil

Beat the eggs on a plate with a little salt and pepper. Soak the bread, cut in three-inch rounds, in the egg on one side only for about ten minutes. Shake off the surplus egg. Cut the Mozzarella into rounds a quarter of an inch thick. Make thick sandwiches with the cheese and the soaked bread, eggy side out, and fasten with toothpicks. Deep fry in olive oil or fry carefully and not too fast in shallow oil, turning once with great care. Take out the toothpicks and drain the sandwiches before eating them.

The cheese melts completely inside a crisp brown crust. In Italy they are eaten with ham inside and also dipped in breadcrumbs before they are fried. Take care that bread is not too thick as the cheese will not melt.

By varying the thickness of the bread you can make a hefty lunch, or a fairly light start to a meal.

For 4

ONION, POTATO AND ANCHOVY GRATIN

2 onions
1 clove garlic, chopped
butter
1 tablespoon olive oil
3 eggs
½ pint milk
1 lb potatoes
10 anchovy fillets
a little cream
salt, if necessary, and freshly ground pepper
cheese (optional)

Make this like the gratin of potatoes and ham (page 88), but instead of ham and cheese, add the anchovies and cream to the potato mixture before you turn it into the gratin dish. Bake as before and finish under the grill. Go easy on the salt because of the saltiness of the anchovies.

You can add cheese to this if you like, using the same quantity as is used in the gratin of ham.

For 4

EGG CURRY WITH TOMATOES, FROM HARVEY DAY'S *CURRIES OF INDIA*

6 eggs, 2 oz butter
2 onions, chopped fine
2 cloves garlic, chopped fine
2 green or red chillies (optional)
½ teaspoon ground coriander
½ teaspoon ground cumin
½ teaspoon (or less) ground chilli
½ teaspoon ground turmeric
3–4 large tomatoes, skinned and chopped
½ oz tamarind (or juice of half a lemon)
salt

Cook this curry in a fireproof dish that you can take to the table. Fry onions, garlic and chillies, deseeded and cut in strips, in the butter, until lightly browned. Add spices and stir for a minute; add tomatoes and ¼ pint warm water. Cook slowly for ten minutes. Stir the tamarind into ¼ pint water, soak for five minutes and strain the resulting juice into the tomato sauce, or add lemon juice. Add salt to taste and return to the boil. Gently break the eggs into the sauce. Serve when they are set, after about five minutes. Eat with lots of bread or rice.

A red-hot chilli and tomato sauce in which you poach the number of eggs you need.

For 3

FROMAGE DES OEUFS

12 eggs
salt
1 pint mayonnaise (page 139)
a few anchovies

Break the eggs into a round flat dish that has been copiously buttered (and lined with buttered grease-proof paper if you want to be extra careful). Be very sure the yolks don't break; although it doesn't spoil the flavour it is not so pretty. Sprinkle a little salt over the eggs and bake in a bain marie in a slowish oven Reg 3½–4/180°, for 35–40 minutes. Allow to cool, turn out, remove the paper and decorate the top with anchovies in a lattice if you like it to be smart. Serve the mayonnaise separately.

This is an alternative way of making egg mayonnaise; the eggs come out in a nice shape like a Brie and you cut it like one. This accounts for the name, as there is actually no cheese in it.

For 6–8

CREAM CHEESE MOUSSE

1 pint consommé (page 12), or 2 tins consommé
8 oz plain cream cheese
2 hard-boiled eggs
salt and freshly ground pepper

Lay the sliced hard-boiled eggs in a white souffle dish. Mix half the consommé, melted, with the cream cheese until it is a smooth cream. Season, pour it over the eggs, and chill until firm. Melt the remaining consommé, but it must be cool when you pour it over the cheese mixture, Chill again.

A very good summer lunch dish with a green salad. Make the day before.

For 6

OEUFS À LA TRIPE

6 hard-boiled eggs
½ pint onion sauce (page 140)

Slice the eggs into thick rounds and cover with hot onion sauce. Serve hot.

For 4

OEUFS À LA SOUBISE

6 hard-boiled eggs
1 lb onions, poached in milk until tender, seasoned and sieved
½ pint creamy, well-flavoured Bechamel (page 137)

Make a mound of onion puree on a hot dish. Place the eggs on top and cover with Bechamel. Serve hot.

For 4

ONION TART

¾ lb button onions (about 36 of them)
2–3 rashers bacon, rinds removed
2 eggs
¼ pint single cream
salt, pepper, and a pinch of nutmeg
9 oz flan pastry (page 172), or less if you like a fragile crust

Preheat the oven to Reg 5/190°. Cook a seven-inch flan case. Trim and peel the little onions, a real labour of love, and cook them whole in boiling salted water for 15–20 minutes. Drain well. Cut the bacon into little strips and fry gently in its own fat. Don't let it become crisp. Arrange the drained onions neatly in the flan case and put little bits of bacon here and there. Beat the eggs with the cream or milk, season with salt, pepper and nutmeg and pour into the tart. Bake it in the moderately hot oven covered with greaseproof paper for 25 minutes; remove the paper and cook five minutes longer to brown the top.

Serve very hot.

If you would rather use larger onions, slice them and saute them in butter for 30 minutes without browning before putting them into the flan case.

For 4–6

QUICHE

1 large onion, finely sliced
1 oz butter
1 teaspoon oil
3 small eggs
½ pint milk
1–2 oz cheese, grated
12 anchovy filiets
salt, if needed, and freshly ground pepper
9 oz flan pastry (page 172)

In the following recipe the filling can be almost anything you like. Instead of onions and anchovies you can put ham or bacon with more cheese; chopped leeks softened in butter, with cheese; cooked crab or shrimps; mushrooms, previously sweated in butter; fresh asparagus with a little cheese; cooked potatoes cut in cubes with ham and chives; a great big panful of softened sliced onions; smoked haddock with a little cheese; or just a really fresh bunch of mixed herbs, finely chopped.

Make a flan case. Keep the oven at Reg 5/190°. Soften the onion in the oil and butter in a small frying pan, without browning. Beat together the eggs, milk and cheese. Put the drained, tender onions in the flan case, lay the anchovies on top and pour on the egg mixture. Bake ten minutes at Reg 5/190°, then another 15–20 at Reg 4/180°. When it is nicely browned and puffed up it is ready. It is better sloppy-ish than overcooked, and pre-cooking the flan case makes sure that the pastry won't be raw. It can be eaten hot or cold, or even tepid, which seems a good temperature for the custard.

For 4 (main course) or 6 (starter)

PASTA, PANCAKES, GNOCCHI, DUMPLINGS AND FRITTERS

Packets of spaghetti in their traditional deep blue paper with red and yellow labels are always an encouraging sight in the larder; as long as they are there, preferably lying alongside a large tin of tomatoes and a can of olive oil, you will never be short of a meal. But the truth is that these packets won't keep for years and, especially in the case of noodles, it is better to eat them within a few months of purchasing or you may find yourself serving a bowl of nicely shredded cardboard. Always choose pasta made in Italy – they do know how to do it there – and always cook it with care, it is so boring once it has gone completely soft. The instructions for cooking pasta (page 44) apply to every kind there is from fettucine, tagliatelli and linguine, which are all types of noodles, to macaroni and cannelloni, which are the larger kinds of pasta. Some of the shapes, such as conchiglie which are shells and ruote, which are wheels, are pretty to have about, but need lots of sauce to make a good dish. Pasta with a sauce, preferably with a heavy aroma of fresh herbs, is a perfect lunch followed by a green salad, cheese and fruit. And if you serve it in the summer on a terrace or under a tree, it can produce a state of euphoria.

Gnocchi are more delicate than pasta and tend to be eaten with less abandon because they cannot be bought but must be freshly made, which seems to give them a touch of luxury although they are a simple form of food. Gnocchi are a wonderful vehicle for sauces and some, such as the green ones, need nothing more than extra butter and Parmesan. They are made with humble ingredients, semolina, potatoes and flour, and so are a very inexpensive meal, but they are rather a fiddle to make.

Pancakes, stuffed with a velvety filling, are a delicious vehicle for the despised left-over; chicken, spinach, smoked haddock, mushrooms, ham, chicken livers, scallops, can each make a good stuffing for a pancake. Bind them in a smooth, not stodgy, well-flavoured sauce, and make the pancakes as thin as possible, light and crisp. As with any other dish that uses left-overs, there is a vital rule to follow: don't be tempted to use more than one in each stuffing. However much you long to get rid of little dishes of sweetcorn and peas sitting neglected in the refrigerator, they will probably bring your pancake down to the mish-mash level.

Dumplings and fritters are often forgotten because they are so plain, and plain cooking is not fashionable. Both are useful and not too taxing ways of extending the possibilities and filling power of ordinary foods, and a stew with light little dumplings swimming in it looks as though somebody really cared about it. Fritters can be quite delicious, especially if made with a very light batter that doesn't hold too much oil (page 56), but it is always vital to drain them really well on kitchen paper. Several vegetables make good fritters; aubergines, courgettes, salsify and sorrel or spinach, dipped a leaf at a time into the egg-white batter, are all excellent. So are mussels, and slices of cheese, not to mention the worthy spam or corned beef fritters, both of which children still admire tremendously.

COOKING PASTA

The difference between pasta cooked well – light, slightly *al dente*, each thread or shape separate – and pasta cooked badly – heavy, glutinous and clinging – is drastic. It's very hard to make a packet of spaghetti that has been hanging about for months taste good, and it should always be bought at a shop that sells plenty of it so it is more likely to be fresh. To produce a perfectionist dish of pasta remember:

1. A teaspoon of butter or oil in the water while the pasta is cooking prevents it from sticking to the pan.

2. Three ounces of dried pasta is enough for one person.

3. Ideally you need two gallons of water to cook one pound of pasta, though less will do.

4. Use one and a half tablespoons of salt to every gallon of water.

5. Stir the water round before you put the pasta in, and again as soon as the pasta is in, and during the cooking to make sure it doesn't stick together.

6. Don't overcook the pasta. It should be *al dente*, with a slight resistance when you bite it, so after ten minutes test it every now and then by biting a piece.

7. When cooked and drained, tip it at once into a large heated dish and stir a little olive oil or butter into it.

8. Serve it as soon as possible to eat it at its best. If it must wait a little while, pour boiling water over it, drain, add butter or oil and keep it warm over a pan of hot water, or in a low oven, covered with a cloth.

9. Serve most sauces separately and have freshly grated Parmesan and more butter on the table, plus copious amounts of rough red wine. People also like plenty of freshly ground pepper and large chunks of bread.

Freshly-made pasta – if you are lucky enough to get it – is cooked in the same way but for less time; start testing it after eight minutes.

SPAGHETTI BOLOGNESE

12 oz spaghetti
3 tablespoons olive oil
1 onion, chopped
¾ lb freshly minced beef, pork, or veal and pork
5 tomatoes, skinned and chopped
1 clove garlic
1 tablespoon tomato puree, diluted with a little water
salt and freshly ground pepper
sprig thyme
small bunch parsley
large pinch basil
Parmesan/freshly grated

Heat the oil in a saucepan, peel and chop the onion and sweat in the oil for five minutes without browning. Turn up the heat and, when the oil is very hot, add the meat and fry fiercely to brown it, stirring all the time to keep it crumbly. Peel the tomatoes, chop them coarsely and add to the meat. Chop the clove of garlic finely and add with the diluted tomato puree, salt, freshly ground black pepper and roughly chopped herbs. Cook gently, uncovered, for ¾–1 hour, stirring from time to time. The sauce will condense considerably and should seem bathed in oil and tomato. Serve on pasta, with grated Parmesan as usual, or use in lasagne or cannelloni.

For 4

SPAGHETTI CARBONARA

¼lb spaghetti or other pasta
3 rashers bacon or slices ham
1 egg
salt and freshly ground pepper
Parmesan, freshly grated

While the pasta is cooking in plenty of boiling water, cut the bacon or ham into thin strips. Put the rinds or pieces of ham fat into the pan on a low heat and when the fat starts to run take them out and add the bacon or ham strips. Let them cook until the bacon is crisp, or the ham sizzling hot; keep hot. Beat the egg, and season with salt and pepper, unless you know the bacon to be very salty.

When the pasta is ready (15–20 minutes), drain and tip it into a very hot serving dish, then quickly add the beaten egg to the hot pasta and stir it about. Add the bacon or ham and the fat it cooked in.

The egg is lightly cooked by the heat of the pasta, but if this seems daunting you can lightly (but very lightly) scramble the egg with the bacon in the pan before pouring it on to the pasta. Sprinkle with cheese and eat it at once.

This is useful if you have no tomatoes or other sauce.

For 2

SPAGHETTI WITH CHICKEN LIVER SAUCE

12 oz spaghetti
3 tablespoons olive oil
1 onion, chopped
2 cloves garlic
1½ lbs tomatoes
parsley, thyme and marjoram, fresh or dried
salt and freshly ground pepper
small glass red wine
¾lb chicken livers
1 tablespoon butter
Parmesan, freshly grated, if liked

Heat the olive oil in a large shallow saucepan. Chop the onion and garlic and sweat them for 15 minutes in the oil without browning. Skin the tomatoes, chop roughly and add them with the wine, salt, pepper and plenty of chopped herbs, and simmer uncovered for about an hour until you have a thickish sauce. Cook the spaghetti. While it is boiling chop the chicken livers into pieces the size of a hazelnut and saute in butter for a few minutes until they are brown on the outside. Add them with their juice to the tomato sauce and serve straight away with the spaghetti, with or without grated cheese.

For 4

SPAGHETTI ALLA PUTTANESCA

12 oz spaghetti
2 red, yellow or green peppers
4 cloves garlic
1–2 oz small black olives
olive oil
Parmesan, freshly grated

Remove every seed from the peppers and cut them into strips. Peel and slice the garlic cloves. Stone the olives if you like. Heat 3–4 tablespoons of olive oil in a sauté pan, and sauté the peppers until they are cooked through, 10–15 minutes. Add the garlic and olives and cook on for three or four minutes, stirring. In the meantime cook the spaghetti in fast-boiling salted water. Drain and put in a large bowl, pour the pepper mixture over and serve with fresh olive oil and grated Parmesan if liked.

'Alla puttanesca' means as a tart would cook it, and it is a very basic dish.

For 4

NOODLES WITH COCKLES

¾ lb spaghetti or 1lb noodles
3 cloves garlic
1 onion, chopped
3 tablespoons olive oil
1lb tomatoes, skinned, de-seeded and chopped
4 sprigs parsley, coarsely chopped
salt and freshly ground pepper
3 pints fresh cockles, well washed (pickled ones are horrible)

Chop the garlic and onions and soften in the oil for 15–20 minutes. Add the tomatoes, parsley, salt and pepper and cook a further five minutes. (The tomatoes should be very lightly cooked for this dish.) Meanwhile cook the noodles or spaghetti in plenty of boiling salted water. Shake the well washed cockles in a thick pan over a low heat until they are open, and then remove from their shells. Add them to the sauce at the last minute and heat through.

No cheese with this dish unless you are fanatic about it, but you can add more chopped parsley and a dab of butter as you serve it.

For 4

NOODLES WITH CRISPY BACON

1 lb packet egg noodles
4–5 rashers bacon, rinds removed
½ pint cream
2 egg yolks
salt and freshly ground pepper
garlic
Parmesan, freshly grated
chives, chopped

Cook the noodles in boiling salted water until they are tender but with a bite. Meanwhile fry the bacon briskly in a dab of butter until it is crisp and brown but not burned. Beat the egg yolks, chives and cream together, add the drained bacon, broken into bits, season if necessary and heat gently in a double boiler until thick enough to coat the back of your spoon. You can add a little crushed garlic if you like. When you have drained the noodles, stir in the bacon mixture, coating the noodles thoroughly, and serve with grated Parmesan, and more chopped chives if you like.

This is an anglicised version of spaghetti carbonara.

For 4–5

NOODLES WITH CREAM AND FRESH HERBS

1 lb egg noodles, fresh if possible
¼ pint cream
parsley
chives
rosemary
2 cloves garlic
4oz butter
salt and freshly ground pepper
Parmesan, freshly grated

Warm the cream. Cook the noodles in boiling salted water until just tender but with a bite. Drain thoroughly. Chop the herbs together coarsely. Stir into the noodles the heated cream, half the butter, the pounded garlic and chopped herbs, and season with salt and plenty of ground pepper. Put a tablespoon of grated Parmesan on top of each plateful of noodles and a good knob of butter on top of that. A plate of these looks particularly good: creamy white with green herbs and a yellow pool of butter in the centre.

As in all spaghetti recipes this sauce can be used on any kind of pasta, but is best on the thinner, more delicate kinds: spaghetti, tagliatelle, linguine etc.

For 6, or 4 as a main dish

LASAGNE

½ lb lasagne
2 onions
2 cloves garlic
olive oil
¾ lb minced pork
¾ lb minced veal
1 lb tomatoes
salt and freshly ground pepper
thyme
stock if necessary
for the sauce:
3 oz butter
3 oz flour
1½ pints milk
2 oz Parmesan, grated
salt and pepper
bayleaf
grating of nutmeg
butter
cheese for sprinkling on the top

Heat the olive oil in a saucepan and fry the chopped onions and garlic. Add the meat and fry until it is browned, stirring all the time. Skin the tomatoes, chop them roughly and add to the meat with the thyme, salt and pepper. Let the tomatoes soften.

If they do not make enough liquid to cook the sauce in, gradually add a little stock, but always a bit less than you think is necessary. Cook the sauce gently, stirring occasionally, for as long as you like, ¾ hour should be enough. Meanwhile cook the lasagne, a few at a time, in a huge pan of boiling well-salted water for 11 minutes, moving them around from time to time to prevent them sticking together. Scoop them out and drain on a cloth.

At the same time make 1½ pints Bechamel sauce flavoured with Parmesan, salt, pepper, a bayleaf and plenty of nutmeg.

Preheat the oven to Reg 3½/170°. When everything is ready remove the bayleaf from the sauce. Put a layer of meat in a buttered gratin dish, add a layer of Bechamel, then a layer of slightly overlapping pieces of lasagne. Add more meat, more Bechamel, more lasagne and finish with a layer of meat covered with Bechamel. Sprinkle the top with cheese, dot with butter and bake for ¾ hour.

This is not worth making for less than six, but is well worth doing for more.

For 6

BASIC SAVOURY PANCAKES (1)

4oz plain flour
1 egg
½ pint milk
salt

Beat the egg thoroughly into the milk. Season the flour and stir in the milk and egg mixture gradually, to make a smooth lump-free batter.

Beat for several minutes with a wooden spoon with the bowl of the spoon turned over, so that the air in the hollow of the spoon gets into the batter, or beat with a balloon whisk or an electric beater.

Allow to stand for two hours before using.

This mixture makes 6–8 pancakes; make it two hours before it is needed.

For method of making pancakes see page 154

SAVOURY PANCAKES (2)

Use the same recipe as before but add two teaspoons of melted butter to the mixture, after you have combined the other ingredients. This makes the pancakes just slightly richer, and they can be put under the grill without drying up.

LAYERED PANCAKES

8 savoury pancakes

Use two kinds of filling. Choose from spinach, chicken, fish, or diced hard-boiled egg and bacon. Alternate the layers, stacking the pancakes up, one on top of another, in a deep dish with the fillings in between.

Cover with a final layer of sauce, cheese is the best for this, and put in a moderate oven to heat through. It is best to use hot sauces and pancakes to cut down the time in the oven as much as possible. Serve cut in slices like a cake.

For 4

CHICKEN PANCAKES

12 large pancakes (page 154)
4oz button mushrooms
1oz flour
1oz butter
½ pint chicken stock, or failing this, milk
salt and freshly ground pepper
½–¾ lb cooked left-over chicken, chopped or pulled into manageable pieces
parsley, chopped
Emmenthal cheese, freshly grated, or ½ pint cheese sauce
butter

Make the pancakes and keep hot. Peel the mushrooms and simmer the peel in the chicken stock. Strain the stock and add the sliced mushrooms, simmer a few minutes more.

Make a white roux of the fl our and butter and add the stock and mushrooms gradually. Season and let the sauce cook slowly for ten minutes. Add the chicken pieces together with any jelly that has set in their dish. Stir in the chopped parsley; season again if necessary. Put a line of the filling into each pancake, and fold in or roll up with the ends open. Lay the pancakes side by side in a gratin dish, and either sprinkle with cheese and melted butter and cook under a slow grill for 15–20 minutes or until hot through, or pour the cheese sauce over and then brown – this prevents them from drying up.

For 6

FISH PANCAKES

8 large pancakes
1oz butter
1oz flour
½ pint milk, or fish stock if you have it
½lb cold cooked fish such as cod or haddock (fresh or smoked), salmon
2oz Parmesan, freshly grated
salt and freshly ground pepper
single cream

Make the pancakes and keep them hot. Make a sauce with the butter, flour and milk, or milk and fish stock. Add the cheese, salt and pepper. Use half the sauce to bind the fish, which must be skinned, boned and flaked. Check the seasoning. Put a line of the fish mixture down the edge of each pancake, roll them up and lay them in a flameproof dish. Pour on the rest of the sauce, with a little cream or top of the milk if available, and grill gently until warmed through and lightly browned.

For 4

SPINACH PANCAKES

These are made like fish pancakes above but with spinach, cooked, drained and chopped, instead of the fish, added to the sauce. You can use frozen spinach but add some grated cheese to the sauce for flavour.

GNOCCHI WITH POTATOES AND PÅTÉ À CHOUX

1 lb potatoes, boiled and sieved dry, with salt and a pinch of nutmeg
½ pint water
1 ½ oz butter, cut in pieces
2oz flour
salt and freshly ground pepper
2 eggs
3 oz Parmesan, grated
¾ pint cheese sauce

Put the water and butter in a pan, bring it to the boil, draw aside and instantly tip in the seasoned flour, beating until the mixture is smooth and leaves the sides of the pan. Beat the eggs lightly and add gradually to the warm mixture, beating all the time. Mix this pate a choux with the sieved, dryish potatoes and half the Parmesan cheese. Make little rolls of about one dessertspoon of the mixture on a floured board. Put a wide shallow pan of salted water on to simmer – boiling will break up the gnocchi. Drop them into the water one at a time.

Do only a few at once to allow for their increasing size. When they are done (after about 10 minutes) they will float to the top. Remove them with a perforated spoon and let them drain on a folded cloth, until they are cool. Make a rich cheese sauce. Butter a gratin dish and lay the gnocchi in it without overlapping. Pour over the sauce, sprinkle with the rest of the Parmesan and put under a medium grill to heat through and brown.

A laborious recipe but the result is delicate and luxurious.

For 6 as a first course, or 4 as a main dish.

GNOCCHI WITH SEMOLINA

½ pint milk
½ pint water
1 onion
bayleaf
5 tablespoons semolina
salt and freshly ground pepper
½ oz butter
3 oz Parmesan, grated
tomato sauce (page 143)

Infuse the milk and water with the sliced onion, bayleaf and salt, simmering very gently for five minutes. Strain and return to the pan. Bring back to the boil and add the semolina, beating with a wooden spoon until smooth. Cook for ten minutes over a moderate heat, stirring often to prevent lumps. Remove from the heat and add 2 oz grated Parmesan, the butter and freshly ground black pepper. Beat thoroughly, then spread the mixture evenly in a flat oiled dish. Cool, and you will find it has set enough to cut in one-inch squares or

rounds. Arrange the gnocchi overlapping on a buttered gratin dish, sprinkle with the remaining Parmesan, dot with butter and put under a hot grill. When brown serve with tomato sauce and more cheese.

Of all gnocchi these are probably the easiest to make at home. They are quite light and have a marvellous flavour.

For 4

GREEN GNOCCHI

1lb spinach, washed and chopped
½ lb Ricotta cheese or cottage cheese, sieved
2 egg yolks
4 tablespoons Parmesan, grated
½ teaspoon salt
1–2 oz flour
melted butter for serving

Cook the spinach in a little salted water for five minutes then drain very well so that the spinach is dry. You can puree the spinach at this point for a finer texture. Mix thoroughly with the Ricotta, egg yolks, half the Parmesan and the salt. Shape into little balls the size of a large marble, rolling them lightly in flour. You can prepare them in advance to this point – they will keep for several hours in a cool place. Then drop them one by one into a large pan of simmering salted water, where they will rise to the surface. After four minutes' gentle simmering, remove them carefully with a perforated spoon. Put in a hot serving dish and serve sprinkled with melted butter and the rest of the Parmesan. They are feathery light, pale green melting globes, a marvellous light lunch or start to a dinner party.

For 4

PARSLEY DUMPLINGS

4 oz plain flour
2 level teaspoons baking powder
½ teaspoon salt
1 oz butter
1 egg
handful of chopped parsley
milk

Mix the flour, salt and baking powder. Cut the butter into small pieces and rub it into the flour. Mix the egg and parsley and stir into the flour mixture. Add milk little by little to make a stiff dough. Form into little balls the size of marbles. Drop them on to the top of your stew, which is already cooking, about 20 minutes before you want to eat. Put the lid on and leave for 20 minutes; they will be twice the size and very light.

Delicious with stews or casseroles of beef or game, as an alternative to potatoes.

For 6

PIZZA DOUGH

1 lb flour
1 oz yeast (or ½ oz freshly bought dried yeast)
1½ teaspoons salt
¼–½ pint water
3 tablespoons olive oil

Dissolve the salt in ½ pint warm water (blood heat or less). Put the flour in a bowl, make a well in the centre and pour in the yeast, dissolved in about two tablespoons of the warm water. Mix with one hand, gradually adding more water with the other. When you have a stringy mass give it a few good turns and nudges, and when it is elastic, springy and not wet put it in a lump in a large bowl, cover with a floured cloth and a lid and leave it to rise for an hour or so, until it has about doubled in size. Take it out, knead it well, then add the oil, working in a small quantity at a time with your hands. When it has absorbed about three tablespoons and is a good pliable, smooth consistency again, make it into three or four nice flat rounds and leave them to prove for 20 minutes. Then put on the sauce, cheese etc. Alternatively put the sauce and cheese on before proving. You don't need to prove before baking, but the pizza may not be so light.

For 4 pizzas

PIZZA

¾ pint well-seasoned tomato sauce made with tinned or fresh tomatoes (page 143)
1 or 2 Mozzarella cheeses
anchovy fillets
black olives, stoned
oregano, basil or marjoram
olive oil
1 lb pizza dough (opposite)

Preheat oven to Reg 6/200°. When the dough has risen and been kneaded, shape it into flat rounds or oblongs the size of the pizza you want to make, and lay them in greased tins. Spread liberally with the tomato sauce and lay slices of cheese, anchovy fillets and black olives on top. Sprinkle with oregano, basil or marjoram and a generous amount of olive oil, about 1 dessertspoon for each small pizza.

Don't take the filling right to the edges, because the crust makes a sort of bank to keep the filling in while it cooks. Leave 20 minutes to rise again. Bake at Reg 6/200° for 15 minutes, then at Reg 5/190° for 15–20 minutes more.

This is a Neapolitan pizza. There are lots of other fillings you can put in a basic pizza, but perhaps the simple olive and anchovy is really the best of all.

3 large or 6 small

OTHER VARIATIONS

American Hot: slices of red pepper sauteed in oil, slices of hot Italian sausage and strips of fresh or bottled chillies on top of the usual tomato and cheese.

Mushroom: mushrooms sliced and lightly sauteed in oil or butter, instead of anchovies and olives.

American Sweet: slices of red pepper sauteed in oil and slices of ordinary salami or sausage, marjoram and the usual tomato and cheese.

Onion: the Neapolitan pizza with lightly fried onion rings strewn on with the anchovies etc.

Aglio e Olio: simply garlic, olive oil and fresh chopped marjoram – no cheese, no tomatoes.

Alla Romana: without tomatoes or anchovies but with sliced Mozzarella, Parmesan and fresh basil.

Mussels: with tomato sauce, oregano, garlic, parsley and little shelled mussels (or clams).

The pizza can also be covered with another piece of dough before baking if full of extra juicy filling, although this can make it stodgy.

NORFOLK DUMPLINGS

8 oz self-raising flour
1 teaspoon salt
water

Sift the flour and salt into a bowl and mix with water to make a dough. Shape the dough into balls during the size of a walnut. A good way of doing this is in the floured palm of your hand. Put in a steamer and steam exactly 20 minutes. Do not remove the lid during cooking time or the dumplings will spoil, and remember that dumplings are like souffles: they will not wait. Called fillers these are served with gravy or butter or brown sugar. Called swimmers they are served with jam or syrup. You can steam these dumplings by sitting them on the top of a dryish stew for 20 minutes, keeping the pot closed.

They are very good, too, with chopped herbs in them, parsley or marjoram.

For 4 or more

SIMPLE FRITTER BATTER

4 oz flour
1 egg
salt
1 tablespoon oil
¼ pint milk, or less

Sieve the flour with a pinch of salt into a bowl, and make a well in the centre. Separate the egg and keep . the white aside. Mix the yolk carefully with the flour, blending well with a wooden spoon. Add the oil and then the milk, a little at a time, drawing in the flour gradually. When you have a thick, smooth, creamy batter stop adding milk and beat the mixture well. Allow it to stand as long as possible in a cool place; about two hours is ideal. Just before you need it, beat the white of the egg stiffly and fold it into the batter.

This is for fritters to be fried in deep oil. If using it for sweet things you can add a spoonful of liqueur to replace some of the milk.

This is good for sweet fritters, or fairly solid things like corned-beef fritters.

Enough for fritters for 4–6 people

DELICATE FRITTER BATTER

4 oz flour
3 tablespoons melted butter
¼ pint lukewarm water
salt
1 egg white

About two hours before it is needed, start the batter. In a bowl mix the flour, a pinch of salt and the melted butter, then add water gradually until you have a thickish creamy mixture. Let it stand in a cool place. At the last moment beat the egg white to soft peaks and fold it into the batter mixture.

Very good for savoury fritters, vegetables etc.

Enough for fritters for 4–6 people

FISH

Fishmongers seem to be a vanishing race, and if you live inland and can find a fish that has been for a swim in the last week, you are lucky. If you do have an excellent fishmonger, or live near the sea and know that the catch has just come in, fish is one of the greatest treats. But it is an absolute must to have fish that is fresh; you can tell by the smell, and by the general glossiness of its condition.

Most books recommend a look at the gills to see how fresh a fish is, but few fishmongers are very agreeable about this; and beware, Tante Marie advises, of those who brighten the gills with lamb's blood just to deceive you (as if they would bother). Anyway fresh fish looks fresh and not at all dingy, and if it is a herring it will be floppy and slippery, if a mackerel stiff and a radiant blue or green. You should always ask the man behind the counter what he recommends. If he wants you to come back he is unlikely to suggest something doubtful.

Shellfish have sadly become more and more expensive, but fresh cockles and mussels really are worth buying (or looking for by the seaside, always checking first that the source is pure), It is no longer so easy to catch your own shrimps, but the small brown British ones, if you can get them, are worth having; although they are fiddly to shell, they have a really good flavour and are lovely for tea with brown bread and butter. Fish from the freezer is second best, for although it is spanking fresh when it goes into the freezing plant, most of it comes out in such unpromising looking doorsteps that it makes dreary material for any recipe.

Besides, it is cheaper to make your own fish fingers and fishcakes, though perhaps a bore, and it is much more pleasurable to buy cod cutlets from a real cod, with luminous golden green freckled skin and actual bones – inconvenience food if you like, but worth it.

The prices of fish whizz up and down with the seasons and weather, but roughly speaking mackerel are best in summer and cheap all the year round, herrings are good all the year round; smoked haddock are less good in spring and early summer, but still better value than a lot of other fish.

Make sure you get undyed haddock on the bone. If it is dyed bright yellow and filleted, you are possibly buying smoked cod, which is cheaper but has a much stronger flavour and is often more salty, which makes it a less useful fish for cooking. Sprats are best in winter and bloaters and kippers (again look for undyed fish) in summer. Cod is expensive in the spring.

This book doesn't mention salmon, turbot, halibut, lobster and so on because they are practically the most expensive food you can buy, unless you have a fisherman in the family.

Lots of people have, but even so fish is generally a neglected form of food – partly, one suspects, because it makes the house smell when it is cooking. If you bake it in the oven, covered with foil, this is not much of a problem. Old-fashioned cooks often baked it in a covered buttered tin with no liquid, and it does stay very succulent cooked like this; it is also worth buying a second-hand fish kettle for the occasions when you want to steam a whole cod or haddock (or salmon-trout if you are in luck) because it makes the operation of getting the fish out of the pan, in one piece, a great deal less tricky. It comes in quite useful, too, for sterilising bottles. About the most useless piece of equipment you could find is a fish-shaped frying pan; because it is so badly balanced it tips over constantly, and it holds no more than an ordinary round pan. A fish-scaler could be useful if you were constantly tearing huge scales off gigantic fish, but this is easily done with a knife, held rather flat against the skin and scraped lightly from tail to head in short strokes.

If you are poaching fish (which is quite different from boiling it) it is the easiest thing to make a delicate court-bouillon. Put in a large pan one part wine vinegar to ten parts water, with plenty of salt, peppercorns, sprigs of parsley and finely sliced onions and carrots, and boil everything for twenty minutes to half an hour before you add the fish. You can also make a quick stock with the heads, bones and trimmings of the fish simmered in water with onion, parsley, salt and peppercorns, to which you add a dash of white wine if you can. Three of the best things to serve with plain poached fish are the herb butters (page 144), Hollandaise sauce (page 138), and a Bechamel (page 137) made partly with the fish stock and coloured brilliant green with handfuls of fresh chopped parsley.

FRESH COD WITH AIOLI

2–3 lbs centre cut of cod (must be fresh)
12 egg-sized potatoes, preferably new, washed but not peeled
6 hard-boiled eggs
1 lb cleaned carrots
6 courgettes,
1lb French beans
6 small green artichokes – if in season, but fish, carrots, potatoes and eggs form a very good dish
aioli (page 136) or melted butter
court-bouillon:
quarts water, ½ pint cider vinegar
1 sliced onion, 1 stick celery, 1 bayleaf, 12 peppercorns

Boil the ingredients for the court-bouillon together for 25 minutes and allow to cool to blood heat. Add two teaspoons of salt. Cook the cod in this by simmering for ten minutes to a pound. Boil or steam the potatoes and other vegetables separately, until just done (avoid overdoing them).

Serve everything on a large dish, each kind of vegetable and the eggs in separate groups, the fish in the centre. Serve with plenty of stinging strong aioli (or melted butter for those who don't like garlic).

An English version of salt cod with aioli, it makes a marvellous weekend lunch, and is very good for a large family.

For 4-6

COD MAYONNAISE WITH CAPERS

1 whole fresh cod weighing about 6 lbs, or 3½ lbs centre cut of cod
court-bouillon (see previous recipe)
½ pint mayonnaise (page 139) made with the caper vinegar
capers

Buy the whole fresh cod on the bone, remove the head and cook this in the court-bouillon in a huge pan or fish kettle for 20 minutes. Allow the court-bouillon to cool to blood-heat, take out the cod's head and put in the rest ofthe fish. Poach it gently with the lid on for 10 minutes per lb. When just cooked, but not falling to pieces, take out the fish and drain it. Remove the skin and flake the flesh from the bones.

Make the mayonnaise with a little caper vinegar and a little wine or cider vinegar, and thin it down with wine vinegar until it is the consistency of thick cream, or use cream or water; add a handful of capers. Pile the cod flakes on a dish, pour the mayonnaise over and chill. Dot the mayonnaise with a few more capers.

For 8–10

COD WITH CHEESE SAUCE

1 cod cutlet per person
1 pint court-bouillon (page 59)
½ pint cheese sauce (see souffle cheese omelette, page 34)
butter
2 tablespoons cheese, grated

Poach the cod steaks gently in the court-bouillon for 15–20 minutes, while you make the cheese sauce. Put half the well-seasoned sauce in the bottom of a gratin dish, then the drained, poached fish. Pour the rest of the sauce over the top, dot with butter, sprinkle with grated cheese and bake in a moderate oven until browned, or put under a gentle grill.

For 2

COD PORTUGAISE

4 cod cutlets
3 tablespoons lemon juice
4 tablespoons olive oil
12 peppercorns
salt
1 bayleaf
1 clove garlic, crushed
½ pint pizzaiola sauce (page 140)
parsley

Make a marinade from the lemon juice, olive oil, peppercorns, salt, bayleaf and crushed clove of garlic. Marinate the fish in this for not less than half an hour, turning once. Drain the cutlets, put them in a buttered oven dish and bake, covered, for half an hour at Reg 4/180°. Heat the pizzaiola sauce, pour some over each piece of fish and return to the oven for ten minutes. Serve sprinkled with freshly chopped parsley.

For 4

FILLETED HERRINGS IN OATMEAL

2 good herrings
handful porridge oats
salt and freshly ground pepper
lard
1 lemon or fresh tomato sauce (page 143)

Mix the oats with salt and pepper on a board or plate and pat them onto the opened, filleted fish. Fry in lard, top first so they end up skin side down. They take about 2½ minutes each side, depending on the size of the fish. Serve with lemon wedges or with fresh tomato sauce.

For 2

STUFFED HERRINGS

4 herrings
4 oz fresh breadcrumbs
1 oz butter, well softened
chopped parsley, savory or tarragon
lemon rind, grated
egg to bind
salt and freshly ground pepper

Remove the scales from the fish. Cut off the fishes' heads, removing the innards at the same time by leaving them attached to the head.

With a very sharp knife, cut the fish open along the backbone, ending at the tail. Smooth your finger along one side of the bone, and the fish falls in half like a book falling open. Hold the tail in one hand, slip the knife under the tail end of the bone to start it off, and pull. The backbone comes out like a zip, all in one piece, if the fish are not frozen stiff. Pick out the remaining bones.

Mix all except the herrings together and season well. Open the herrings, remove the backbones, put the stuffing inside, press together lightly and bake in a moderately low oven, Reg 3/160°, for half an hour.

A lot of people object to eating herrings because of all the spiky little bones that seem to get in every mouthful. It is very easy to take the bones out and you are left with a very good fish.

For 4

MARINATED MACKEREL WITH MARJORAM

6 mackerel
3 bayleaves
glass white wine or cider
¼–½ pint cider vinegar or wine vinegar
¼–½ pint water
sprigs of marjoram, orfailing this oregano or parsley
12 peppercorns
salt

Get the fishmonger to fillet the mackerel, or do it yourself. Cut the fillets in two lengthwise. Roll the fillets up from the tail end and put in a fireproof dish all facing the same way and with all the silver to one side and the dark blue to the other. Pour over the wine and vinegar. Add enough water to cover. Put in the marjoram and peppercorns and a little salt and cook in a very slow oven, Reg 2/150°, for one hour. Allow to cool, when they will set in a nicely-flavoured jelly.

You can also do this with herrings.

For 6

MACKEREL STUFFED WITH GOOSEBERRIES

1 mackerel per person
1 or 2 oz gooseberries per mackerel
salt and freshly ground pepper
sugar

Simmer the gooseberries in a little water, mashing while they cook, until you have a puree. Season generously with salt, pepper and sugar.

Fillet the fish (see page 66) leaving them joined along the belly. Open them flat and spread the puree on one side. Press the fish together again, lay in a buttered dish and cover with greased paper, or wrap them individually in foil parcels. Bake in a moderate oven, Reg 4/180°, for 30 minutes or longer, depending on the size of the fish.

KIPPER SALAD

2 fresh, undyed uncooked kippers
oil
1 lemon
1 small onion, sliced thinly into rings
1 large cold cooked potato, peeled and diced
1 green pepper (optional), seeded and diced
salt, freshly ground pepper and a pinch of paprika
parsley, chopped

Skin and bone the uncooked kippers; this is quite easy if they are fresh and juicy. Cut them into small squares, and cover with oil and the juice of half the lemon while you prepare the other ingredients. Put a dressing of oil and lemon, salt and pepper on the potatoes. Mix the onion and green pepper with the kipper.

Serve the kipper salad sprinkled with parsley and the potato salad sprinkled with paprika, side by side.

For 2

SEVICHE

1 lb sea-bass or other firm-fleshed fish, boned and cut into half-inch cubes
1 onion, chopped
1 small green pimento, finely chopped
juice of 2 lemons (or limes if you can get them)
1 small green chilli, finely chopped
1 tablespoon olive oil
handful of fresh parsley, finely chopped
salt

Mix all the ingredients together well and put them in a covered bowl in the refrigerator overnight. That's it; eat it raw. It is "cooked" by the action of the lemon or lime juice, but the trick is not to mention this until after people have eaten it. The fish must be very fresh.

A Latin-American dish.

For 6

KEDGEREE (1)

1½ lbs smoked haddock on the bone
½ pint milk
½ pint water
12 oz rice
2 oz flour
1½ oz butter
tablespoons cheese, grated, or ½ teaspoon curry powder
3 hard-boiled eggs

Poach the haddock gently in milk and water until the flesh comes off the bones easily (after about ten minutes). Keep aside the liquid in which it is cooked. Wash the rice and boil in plenty of salted water for

minutes; drain and wash it well. Make a sauce with the flour, butter and haddock liquid. If you like a slight curry flavour, cook the powder in the butter for a few moments before adding the flour.

If you prefer cheese, leave out the curry and add the cheese to the sauce. It should be fairly thick, but the rice will absorb some of it, so if you like sloshy kedgeree, make the sauce thinner by adding more milk.

Add the flaked fish, chopped hard-boiled eggs and cooked, drained rice. Put the mixture in the top of a double saucepan and steam for 20–30 minutes.

Serve with a lump of butter on each helping.

For 4–6

KEDGEREE (2)

½ lb cooked smoked haddock
6 oz cooked rice
3 hard-boiled eggs, chopped or sliced
handful cooked peas orchopped parsley
butter
salt or freshly ground pepper
2 tablespoons cream

Combine these ingredients in the top of a double boiler, adding the chopped hard-boiled eggs last of all, and stir very gently a couple of times while you heat it through.

A very good breakfast dish.This is a dryish kedgeree, but the moisture in the rice and the fish, and plenty of butter or a couple of tablespoons of cream, give it a good succulent consistency.

For 4

CREAMED SMOKED HADDOCK

1 lb smoked haddock on the bone
½ pint milk
1 oz butter
½ oz flour
2 tablespoons Parmesan, grated (optional)
plenty of freshly ground pepper
salt if necessary

Poach the haddock in the milk until it comes easily off the bone – about ten minutes, taking care not to let it burn at the bottom, and then strain the milk into a jug. Remove the skin and bones, and shred the fish as finely as possible with a knife and fork, or sieve through the coarse disc of the mouli, or liquidise for a few seconds.

Make a sauce with the butter, flour and the milk in which the fish was cooked. Add the cheese, pepper and the fish. Taste for salt.

Serve the purée on golden fried bread cut in triangles.

Good for a first course or for supper with a poached egg on top.

For 2

FISH PIE

¾ lb smoked haddock
¾ lb fresh haddock
1 ½ lbs potatoes, boiled and mashed with plenty of butter and milk
½ oz butter
1 ½ oz flour
¾ pint milk
½ pint water
1 teaspoon white wine- or cider-vinegar
salt and freshly ground pepper
3 hard-boiled eggs
parsley, chopped

Preheat the oven to Reg 5/190°. Poach the fish in the milk and water for 15 minutes, or until the skin and bones come away easily, basting with the liquid a couple of times. Make a sauce with the butter, flour and enough of the fish liquid to give it the consistency of double cream. Add the vinegar, seasoning, flaked fish, sliced eggs and parsley to the sauce. Arrange the mixture in a pie dish and cover with mashed potato. Dot with butter and bake at Reg 5/190°, for half an hour or until brown. This pie is very much liked by children; if it is for adults you can add chopped scallops sauteed in butter, for the brief glorious couple of months they are in season, but it is excellent anyway.

For 6

FISH CAKES

1½ lbs cod, hake or fresh haddock
4–5 large potatoes, baked and mashed dry
2 hard-boiled eggs
for the sauce:
1½ oz butter, 1½ oz flour
¾ pint milk infused with 1 carrot, 1 onion and some parsley for 30 minutes
salt and freshly ground pepper
for coating and deep-frying:
1 beaten egg
dried breadcrumbs
lard, oil or dripping

Bake the potatoes, then skin and mash them. Cook the fish in a covered greased dish in a medium oven, Reg 4/180°, until the bones and skin come away easily. Remove the skin and bones, flake the fish. Make a stiffish sauce with the butter, flour and flavoured milk, plus any liquid given out by the fish while it cooked. Mix the potato, fish, chopped hard-boiled eggs and sauce. Season and leave to cool, preferably overnight. When cold make small, round flat cakes or cork shapes; roll them in flour and pat smooth.

Dip into beaten egg, then breadcrumbs, and fry three or four minutes in hot deep fat. Drain on kitchen paper.

For 8–10

FISH SOUP (BOUILLABAISSE)

2 lbs mixed fish and shellfish as available
2 onions, 3 cloves garlic, 1 bayleaf
large sprigs thyme, parsley, and fennel (use bulb fennel or seeds if no fresh)
2 tomatoes, 1 strip orange peel
large pinch saffron, salt and pepper
4 tablespoons olive oil, dash of white wine
Parmesan, grated, rouille (page 141)
4 slices of French bread dried slowly in the oven

Cut the cleaned fish into two-inch pieces. Make a stock with the remains while you crush the garlic, and peel and chop the onions and tomatoes. Put the vegetables in a pan with the garlic, herbs, orange peel, seasoning, saffron and oil. Cook for five minutes without browning. Put the coarser varieties of fish in with the vegetables and strain the boiling stock over them. They should be covered, so add water if necessary and a dash of white wine. Boil fast for five minutes, add the more delicate fish and boil for another five to ten minutes. Add the shellfish five minutes before the end. Serve with toasted bread, a good stinging rouille (page 141) and grated Parmesan cheese.

For 4

SQUID RISOTTO

2 lbs squid
1 small onion, sliced
1 clove garlic, sliced
olive oil
1 wineglass red wine
1 glass warm water
1 small tin tomato puree
salt and freshly ground pepper
10 oz Italian rice

Peel the skin from the body of the squid, pull off the head and with it come the entrails. Take out the bone from the body and cut the tentacles from the head; throw away head, bone and innards. Slice the body into thin rings, chop up the tentacles, and wash well to get rid of any sand.

Fry the onion and garlic in oil in a saute pan with a lid; add the pieces of well-washed squid. Let it stiffen and become less transparent; add the wine, let it simmer for five minutes and add salt, pepper and the tomato puree, plus a glass of warm water. Cover the pan, turn the heat right down and simmer for one hour. Add the rice, well washed under running water, stir from time to time and cook until tender, 20–30 minutes, adding more warm water if it becomes dry. Correct the seasoning and serve.

For 4

DEEP-FRIED SPRATS

1 lb sprats
deep-frying oil (use a whole bottle, strain it after each time you use it and keep it for fish)
seasoned flour
1 lemon

Wash the sprats and pat them dry in a piece of kitchen paper. Flip each one in a heap of seasoned flour, shaking off the surplus before dropping them one by one into hot oil, with a blue haze (not smoke) rising; when pale gold they are done. Drain off the oil as you take them out and keep the fish hot on a paper-lined dish in a low oven.

Remove the paper, and serve them, complete with heads and tails, with lemon wedges. If you haven't had sprats before they will be a great discovery; they are simply delicious fried like this. If you are finicky about bones you can split the sprats before flouring and remove the backbones, leaving heads and tails on; they will fry a fraction faster.

For 4

GRILLED MUSSELS

1 quart mussels
1–2 oz salted butter
3 cloves garlic, finely chopped
handful fresh parsley, finely chopped

Wash the mussels in cold water to clean off the worst of the mud. Cut off the beards, stray limpets (best banged with the back of a knife) and spots of mud. Wash again in clear cold water.

Bring about an inch of water to the boil in a large pan. Throw in the mussels and cook, covered, over a high heat, shaking the pan a couple of times, until they are all opened. It only takes a few minutes. Meanwhile chop the parsley and garlic finely and mash them into the butter with a fork. When the drained opened mussels are cool enough to handle, remove the empty half of each shell and put a hazelnut of garlic butter on each mussel. Put them in a grill pan under a moderate grill until the butter is bubbling hot; serve with plenty of bread to mop up the juice. About 12 mussels each is plenty. They are rather like juicy snails.

For 2

WINKLES AND COCKLES

Gather the winkles from a part of the beach that is known to be clean and pure. Try to take some clean sea water home, to cook them in. Wash them well under a running tap, scrambling them round with your hand, to remove all the mud and sand.

Put a pan of well-salted water or sea water, deep enough to cover the winkles, on to boil. When the water comes to the boil throw them in and turn the heat up. When it returns to a full boil, let them cook for one or two minutes, then drain and run under the cold tap to cool.

Eat them with a pin or toothpick, removing their little black lids before you dexterously hook them out. Some people put vinegar on, but it is not an improvement. They are very good for tea with bread and butter.

Wash cockles well, as for winkles. Bring some *well-salted* water to the boil. Throw in the cockles, turn the heat to moderate and watch carefully. As soon as they open take them out. Very good with drinks taken out of their shells, and with a squeeze of lemon and a sprinkling of parsley.

FRIED COCKLES

2 quarts fresh cockles
2 lemons
masses of freshly ground black pepper
a little salt
olive oil for frying

Wash and dry the cockles very thoroughly.

Heat two or three tablespoons of oil in a large frying pan. Drop the cockles in, stir them round until they open, then smother them in freshly ground pepper and the juice of two lemons. Hardly any salt is needed. Eat straight away.

In Spain these are served with drinks.

For 6–8

COCKLE AND MUSSEL RISOTTO

1 quart each of cockles and mussels
2 tablespoons olive oil
1 medium onion, chopped
8 oz Italian rice
½ glass white wine
1 large pinch saffron
1 red pimento, chopped

As you are going to use the liquid from the shell-fish to cook the rice, it is very important to wash them thoroughly. Since they are full of salty water, do not add any more salt to the cooking water.

Take a large pan with a lid. Bring to the boil sufficient water to come half way up the cockles and mussels. Throw them in, put on the lid and shake the pan once or twice. After five minutes they should all be opened; strain off the liquid and remove most of the shells. Keep the shellfish warm in their liquid while you cook the rice.

Heat the olive oil in a wide shallow pan and cook the chopped onion in it for about 10 minutes without browning; add the rice and stir it round until it becomes transparent.

Dissolve the saffron in the wine, if using powder, or soak the strands in it, and add to the rice. Stir until the rice has absorbed most of the wine. Taste the shellfish liquid and if it is too salt dilute it with fresh water. Pour about half a pint on to the rice, stir it about and add the chopped red pimento. Cover the pan and let the rice simmer, adding more liquid as necessary. When the rice is tender, stir in the shelled cockles and mussels, heat through and pile into a heated dish. Decorate the top in a haphazard way with the cockles and mussels left in their shells.

This can be made with either cockles or mussels or with both.

For 4

PÂTÉS, TERRINES, PIES AND BRAWNS

Pâtés, terrines and pies are all quite considerable tests of cooking ability, because although mincing up the meat and putting the thing together is all quite straightforward, it is the blend of flavours that demands judgement, and the appearance that makes it appetising or not. But even an ugly-looking home-made pâté is a very useful thing to have around, and it should keep for a week in the refrigerator. Ideally the finished pâté should be nicely browned outside, still pink inside (salt pork included in the mixture helps) and enclosed in a good clear layer of jelly or some crisp brown pastry. When you are very practised you can marble each slice with cubes of pork back fat, fillets of the meat you are using, and perhaps pistachio nuts or pieces of ham or tongue layered through the mixture in carefully placed lines, so that each slice gets its share.

The meat is flavoured with a balanced selection of thyme, garlic, juniper berries, bay, mace, lemon-peel, peppercorns, salt, white wine and brandy. Once you have experimented with these you will know what you like using most, and will be unlikely to end up with what is too frequently offered, even in France, a boring sort of meat-loaf.

It is a great triumph if you can get your butcher to mince the meat for you every time, but if not, an electric automatic chopper is a great help in making pâté and potted meat, as it really chops the meat instead of squeezing and grinding it. Otherwise it is the mincer and plenty of energy, and apart from this the only equipment necessary is a terrine or bowl that will go in the oven. Potted meats are best made and potted in small quantities, so small, straight-sided, round white cocotte dishes are useful for this. Potted meat and fish have very rightly had a revival recently – they used to be one of the staple British breakfast foods – and are a very useful way of storing cold ham, tongue, smoked fish or almost any sort of game until you can face eating it again. Don't serve potted meat too chilled, as the butter it contains makes it rather solid and difficult to spread. It is a great treat for tea on hot buttered toast, or even as a first course to a meal.

The recipes in this section include one for pork pie, which is tremendously fiddly to do, so don't be surprised if the first one you make looks a bit strange; it gets better with practice, and it is a lovely thing to be able to produce at a picnic. Of course you can perfectly well buy pork pies, but that is about the limit of charcuterie in this country. You can't always buy interesting pâtés and rillettes or brawns, or things set in jelly or specially good salads made with calves' heads, so you just have to make them if you want them. Luckily they nearly all use the cheaper pieces of meat and are inexpensive provided you don't count the cost of your time.

CHICKEN LIVER PÂTÉ

½ lb chicken livers, frozen or fresh
1 small shallot, chopped very finely
1 oz butter
2 sage leaves, chopped very finely, or ½ teaspoon thyme leaves
1 small clove garlic, mashed
salt and freshly ground black pepper
dash of port, sherry or brandy, or a little white wine

Sort through the chicken livers, washing and drying thoroughly, removing strings and yellow areas. Chop into small pieces and sprinkle with salt and pepper while you fry the shallot in a small saucepan in the butter, without browning. Add the seasoned chicken livers, herbs and garlic, and increase the heat a little, stirring constantly with a wooden spoon. The livers will crumble as you do this. Keep mashing and add the wine, brandy or other alcohol. When all the livers have become pinkish brown (after about five minutes), remove from the heat and continue mashing until the whole thing is smooth. Put into a little souffle dish, or individual cocotte dishes and serve well chilled.

If the pâté is to be kept for several days, pour melted butter on top.

For 4

PIG'S LIVER PÂTÉ

12 oz pig's liver
4 oz salt (preferably) or fresh belly of pork
1 onion
1 clove garlic
salt, freshly ground pepper, pinch mixed spice
small glass white wine
small glass water
1 pig's foot, split in half
rosemary, bayleaf, thyme and parsley, tied together with a thread
bacon fat

Mince the pig's liver and pork with half the onion. Crush the garlic and add it to the meat with the mixed spice, pepper, and salt if using fresh pork. Put the liver mixture into a large terrine and press down evenly. Pour in the water and wine which should cover the meat by half an inch. Slice up the carrot and remaining onion, and lay them on top of the pâté with the herbs and pig's trotter. Cover the dish with foil and bake in a bain-marie at Reg 2/150° for three hours. Remove the trotter, herbs and vegetables. When cold pour melted bacon fat over the top to seal it. Eat cold the following day when the jelly will be set.

Very spicy pâté with a good jelly round it.

Makes 1 lb pâté, for 8–12 people

RABBIT PÂTÉ

1 lb boned rabbit
½ glass white wine
the rabbit liver
1 clove garlic
6 oz streaky bacon rashers, cut thin
salt and freshly ground pepper
grated lemon peel
nutmeg
1 teaspoon fresh thyme leaves

Marinate the best parts of the rabbit meat, cut in little fillets, in the wine, while you mince the rest of the meat and the liver as finely as you can. Chop the garlic and the bacon, rinds removed, as finely as possible, keeping three or four rashers on one side. Add the chopped bacon and garlic to the meat and season with salt, pepper, a pinch of grated lemon peel, nutmeg and thyme. Press the mixture into a suitable earthenware dish in layers with the fillets. Press flat and cover with the reserved rashers of bacon. Pour over the wine marinade and cover the dish with buttered foil. Place in a bain-marie and cook in a slow oven, Reg 2/150°, for two to three hours. It is done when the pâté shrinks from the sides of the dish. Press with a weight while it cools and sets. Eat cold. This pâté improves with keeping and will last up to a week in the refrigerator.

For 6

A RAISED PORK PIE

1 lb lean end of belly of pork, or blade (about three parts lean to one part fat)
salt and freshly ground pepper
water, dried sage
½ pint stock made with 1 pig's trotter and the trimmings from the pork
for the pastry:
12 oz plain flour, pinch salt 4 oz lard
¼ pint water, 1 egg yolk (for glaze)

Trim the meat, mince half of it as finely as you can and chop the other half into pea-sized pieces; it takes a long time. Season well, add sage to your liking and moisten with half a wine glass of water. Preheat the oven to Reg 8/235°.

To make the pie-crust:

Sift the flour with the salt and put to keep warm in a large bowl. Melt the lard, cut in pieces, in the water in a small saucepan, and then bring to the boil; as it boils pour it on to the flour. Mix rapidly with a wooden spoon until it is smooth. Reserve a quarter of the pastry for the lid, keeping it warm. Flatten out the rest as soon as it is cool enough to handle. When it is about quarter to half an inch thick, mould it into a pie shape on the bottom of a large greased jam or storage-jar. Lift it, jar and all, on to a greased baking tin, wait until the crust is cool, and gently ease the jar away. It may collapse a bit, but never mind. You should have a case about five inches in diameter and two or three inches high. Fill the case with the meat, pressing it down well; roll out a lid from the last piece of pastry, and damp the edges with water before sealing it on very carefully. Press the edges together with your fingers and decorate them by indenting with the back of a knife at half-inch intervals or by forking. You can decorate the pie with pastry trimmings cut into leaves and flowers. Tie a band of oiled greaseproof paper round the pie. Paint the top with egg yolk, and make a round hole in the middle for the steam to escape and to pour the juice through.

Bake in the centre of a hot oven for half an hour and then turn the heat down to Reg 5/190° and cook for another hour. Remove the pie and allow it to cool a little. Strain the pig's foot stock and reduce to about ¼ pint. Season with salt, take it off the heat and pour it on to half a teaspoon of gelatine in a jug to make sure it sets. Stir and allow to cool a little. Fill the pie with this liquid, using a small funnel. Let it set and keep the pie overnight if possible. Eat it cold.

For 6–8 people

CORNISH PASTIES

10 oz steak, well trimmed and cut up very small
1 small potato, peeled and cut up small
1 onion, peeled and chopped finely
parsley, chopped finely
salt and freshly ground pepper
3 tablespoons gravy, stock or water
¾ lb shortcrust pastry made from 8 oz plain flour, 3½ oz fat, pinch salt and water to bind
1 egg, beaten, or milk, to glaze pastry

Preheat oven to Reg 7/220°. Mix the steak, potato, onion, parsley, salt and pepper, and moisten with the liquid. Roll out the pastry and cut out six circles with the help of a saucer. Put a dollop of the mixture on the centre of each, brush round the edges with beaten egg or milk, and fold the pastry up pinching the edges together in a pretty serpentine pattern. Place on a greased tin, brush with more beaten egg or milk, prick the tops with a fork to let out the steam and bake in the top. of the oven for 10–15 minutes to cook the pastry; then turn the oven down to Reg 2/150°, and depending on the quality and tenderness of the steak, bake for a further 1 hour. To reheat, put for 15 minutes in a low oven.

6 smallish pasties

POTTED TONGUE OR HAM

8 oz cooked tongue or ham
8 oz butter (cheapest unsalted), clarified (page 173)
½ level teaspoon mace
freshly ground pepper
salt if necessary

Chop up the meat and put in the liquidiser, with 5 oz melted clarified butter, the mace and pepper. Make a fine purée (if you don't have a liquidiser you can do this by pounding it in a pestle and mortar), taste for salt. Pack it into a pot, pressing well down to eliminate air. Chill for half an hour and when firm smooth the top and cover with melted, clarified butter; what is left will just about do the trick. The potted meat is a beautiful pink and should be put in a neutral coloured pot, white, cream or beige to look its best, with the yellow butter in a layer over the top.

Makes 1 lb, for 8–12

RABBIT IN JELLY

1½ lbs rabbit cut in pieces
1 large onion, sliced
1 pig's foot, split
1 bunch parsley
1 lemon
small glass white wine if available
salt and 6 peppercorns

Put the rabbit pieces in a large pan with the sliced onion, pig's foot, a few sprigs of the parsley, a strip of lemon peel, wine, a little salt and the peppercorns. Just cover with cold water, bring to the boil, skim, and simmer very slowly, covered, for about 1½ hours, until the meat comes off the bones easily. Strain and return the liquid to the pan with the pig's trotter. Put in a fresh piece of lemon peel and simmer, uncovered, until the liquid is reduced to one pint. Skim, and flavour with lemon juice and more salt if necessary. Strain the liquid, skim again and add a good handful of chopped parsley. Put the rabbit meat pulled from the bones and the pink inside pieces of the pig's foot (scarcely visible little scraps of delicious meat) into a square or oblong earthenware dish. Pour the liquid over the meat and chill. It will keep three or four days in the refrigerator. For a very firm jelly dissolve a leaf of gelatine, or half an ounce of powdered gelatine, in the liquid, before you add the parsley. Instead of the parsley you can put half a cucumber, cut into small cubes, into the dish with the meat, but as the cucumber is watery the jelly will not stay firm quite as long.

Ideal for a cold lunch on a summer day.

For 4–6

GALANTINE OF BREAST OF VEAL

3 lbs breast of veal, boned (keep the bones)
6 oz minced pork, or sausage meat
6 oz ham or tongue, or 3 oz of each
1 small onion, finely chopped, softened in butter
1 small glass white wine
salt, pepper, parsley, thyme
1 oz butter
½ pint stock
2 onions, chopped
2 carrots, chopped
bouquet garni
for prettiness: truffles or pistachio nuts (optional)

Using the veal bones and whatever else you like, make a stock while you prepare the stuffing.

Cut the ham or tongue into small pieces, but don't mince. Mix into the minced pork or sausage meat, season well, add herbs, wine, softened onions and truffles or pistachio nuts. Spread the mixture on

the boned veal and roll it up. Tie it up with easily seen thread, leaving long ends. Melt the butter in a flameproof casserole, brown the rolled veal all over, remove it and put in the chopped onions, carrots and bouquet garni. Let them sweat for several minutes, then add stock to cover the vegetables, replace the meat, bring the liquid to the boil, cover and continue cfooking in the oven at Reg 2/150° for two hours, basting occasionally. When it is ready remove the meat and leave it to cool. Untie it and spoon a little of the cooking liquid over the meat, just before it sets, to give it a shine. Repeat this basting several times.

Serve cold in neat slices with salad.

For at least 10

BLOATER OR KIPPER PÂTÉ

1 bloater, or 1 kipper
2–3 oz softened butter
lemon juice
salt and freshly ground pepper
pinch cayenne or nutmeg

Pour boiling water over the fish and let it stand for ten minutes. Remove the flesh from the bones and pound, mince or liquidise, adding butter, lemon juice and seasoning. Mix to a fine paste, and remove any whiskery bones left sticking out. Pack into little pots and fork the top. Chill until needed; it keeps several days in the refrigerator.

For 4

BUCKLING PÂTÉ

2 smoked buckling, or 1 smoked mackerel
2 slices white bread, crusts removed
milk
1 clove garlic
2–3 oz butter, softened
juice of ½ lemon
salt and freshly ground pepper

Remove the skin and all the visible bones from the fish. Soak the bread in milk and squeeze dry. Pound the garlic in a pestle and mortar, add the bread and the fish. Pound thoroughly, removing any little bones you may have missed before. Add the butter and lemon juice, plenty of pepper and some salt if necessary. Pound again, pack the mixture into little pots, and chill. Serve with hot toast and butter.

This keeps several days in the refrigerator. It is surprisingly rich and a little goes a long way, but it is quite delicious and very easy to make. If you have a liquidiser you can make it even more rapidly.

For 4

MEAT

Always be extra nice and good-tempered in the butcher's shop; it really is worth being good friends with the man who sells you your meat. He is the person to steer you clear of bargain cuts that are a maze of bones and gristle, he will show you both sides of a piece of stewing steak before wrapping it up. He will advise you which piece of the animal would be most suitable, if you tell him what you want the meat for. He is also more likely to be prepared to do tedious work in the way of boning, mincing and cutting a joint just so, if he is your friend and sees that you care, and if you make a point of going into the shop when it is not particularly busy.

When choosing meat there are several things to bear in mind. Most carcasses have been frozen or chilled but reach the shop soon after slaughter, arid in this short time the freezing, which is done fast and at a very low temperature, does not affect the juiciness of the meat. But what you do not want to carry home in your shopping bag is something that has been sitting in cold storage for weeks; nothing dries meat up so thoroughly, and the fat becomes granular.

New Zealand lamb has of course been frozen, but it is increasingly good as transport gets faster, and is particularly worth buying from October to Christmas, when their lambs are slaughtered and at their best. English lamb, which is slaughtered between three and five months old, is in season from May or even earlier in the year, to September/October; it is expensive but absolutely the best there is.

Avoid any butcher who has everything in the shop already hacked into tiny pieces; these pieces get drier and stringier with every hour they sit around. Better to make for the shop that has whole carcasses hanging up, even if it means waiting a bit longer for the piece you want. Beware also of any chops, steak or liver pre-packed in a cardboard tray; it may be convenient to carry home, but it will have extracted every last drop of juice from the meat by the time it gets there. Since the true art of butchery seems to be on the wane, it is as well to be equipped with the knowledge of a few boning methods, and the equipment with which to do it. A cleaver may make an unsuitable wedding present, but it

is useful if you have forgotten to ask the butcher to cut up the bones and find they won't go in the pan; the flat sides can be used for beating steaks, pork fillet etc. A boning knife, having an extremely tough, narrow blade, can be slipped easily round complicated bones to pare away all the meat. A good sharpener and a set of straight-sided, sharp-pointed French knives, a carving knife and fork, plus some metal skewers for securing boned meat are the only other vital pieces of equipment, but a ham knife is useful if you are in the habit of buying large hams or pieces of gammon.

Keep your knives razor sharp (a carbon steel is very good for this) and have them re-ground if possible about once a year. Little tungsten-steel wheel knife-sharpeners are not recommended because they leave a thin fragile edge that bends over as soon as you use any pressure. Table-sharpeners and electric knife-sharpeners are fine, provided you use them with care. When using a steel, keep the blade of the knife rather flat against it or you will be bending the edge backwards and forwards with every stroke, and weakening it. Carbon steel knives are still the easiest to sharpen; keep them bright with scouring powder and a cork or with harsh plastic wool.

Some offal, for example fry and chitterlings, is hard to buy and disappearing fast, especially in the South of England, where it is also almost impossible to buy mutton.

Stews, daubes and casseroles almost always make use of the cheaper cuts of meat, which are best bought in a piece and cut up at home, when every morsel of sinew and gristle can be carefully trimmed away; these stringy bits never really become tender and make an otherwise good stew seem less of a treat.

Shin, oxtail, ox-tongue and salt-beef, especially brisket, are often disappointingly tough and the reason is almost always the same – undercooking; they must be simmered very gently for up to four hours or even longer, and plenty of time must be allowed for this. Since most daubes and casseroles reheat well, it is a very good idea to cook them the day before, so hungry people won't be kept waiting about for the oxtail to get tender.

It also gives you a chance to remove all the fat from the top, before reheating. This fat, clarified, can sometimes be used for dripping.

AITCHBONE OF BEEF

This is a very large joint, consisting of rump, topside, silverside and brisket. While the quality of the meat on this cut is not as fine as best rump, fillet or sirloin, it costs less than half as much per pound, and is very well worth buying for large family dinners or informal parties. It can be eaten hot or cold.

A small aitchbone weighing ten pounds will feed at least ten people; when trimmed it will weigh about eight pounds. Keep the bones and trimmings removed by the butcher to make stock.

Preheat oven to Reg 7/220°. Rub the aitchbone with oil and garlic if liked. Put into the very hot oven, reducing the heat to Reg 4/180° after 20 minutes. Cook 2¼ hours, basting from time to time. There is a large amount of dripping from this joint for roast potatoes, and very good juices for gravy; because it is such a large joint it is juicier.

Serves 10–15 according to size

BOILED BEEF AND CARROTS

5 lbs salt beef (brisket or silverside) tied firmly with string
1½–2 lbs large carrots, scraped and halved
3–4 Spanish onions, peeled
3–4 turnips, peeled
bouquet garni
a few peppercorns
dumplings (see page 53) (optional)

Always check with the butcher to see if the beef needs soaking, and if so soak overnight. Put it in a large saucepan with any bones that the butcher may have included, barely cover with cold water and bring it slowly to the boil. Skim thoroughly and add half the vegetables and the herbs and peppercorns. Cover and simmer very gently for 2½–3 hours, longer if the meat is particularly tough. Taste the liquid occasionally, and if it is too salt add more water.

Cook the potatoes and fresh vegetables in with it for the last 25–30 minutes and, if you like, add dumplings too.

Serve the beef with the freshly cooked vegetables, dumplings and some of the broth in which it cooked. Keep the rest of the broth for soup.

For 8

BRISKET IN BEER

3–4 lbs brisket of beef, rolled and tied (fresh, not salted)
6 slices streaky bacon
1 lb onions, sliced finely
½ pint brown ale, ½ pint good stock and ½ pint wine vinegar, heated together
salt and pepper
bayleaf

Take a casserole with a lid, large enough to hold all the ingredients. Line the bottom of it with the bacon, then put in the meat, pack the onions all around, add salt and pepper and the bayleaf. Pour over the stock, beer and vinegar, heated first. Cover tightly and cook at Reg 1½/145° for 3–3½ hours. This is very good cold and the remaining stock makes delicious soup.

For 6–8

CARBONNADE FLAMANDE

1¾ lbs chuck steak
dripping
2 large onions, finely sliced
½ pint Guinness or brown ale
salt and freshly ground pepper
bayleaf, sprig of thyme, pinch nutmeg

Cut the trimmed beef into large cubes. Heat the dripping in a flame-proof casserole, and brown the meat really well all over, so that it has quite a crust on the outside. Remove the pieces to a dish and add the finely sliced onions to the dripping, adding more if necessary. Fry several minutes until the onions are nicely browned. Remove them and put them with the beef while you pour in three-quarters of the beer; let it froth up, scraping the bottom of the pan with a wooden spoon until you have loosened all the sediment. Return the beef and onions, add salt, pepper, herbs and nutmeg and simmer covered on top of the cooker, or in a slow oven, Reg 2/150°, for 2½–3 hours, adding a little water if the gravy gets too thick.

Five minutes before serving add the rest of the beer, taste for seasoning and simmer five minutes more. Serve with boiled potatoes and drink beer with it.

A salad of lettuce eaten off the same plate afterwards benefits from the juices of the carbonnade.

For 4–5

A VERY SIMPLE BEEF STEW

3 lbs stewing beef, leg or chuck
4 oz flour
salt and freshly ground pepper
1 pint best beef stock, or plain water
oil and dripping to brown the meat
24 button onions
24 slender carrots
½ lb button mushrooms (optional)

Trim any fat from the meat and cut it into cubes. Season the flour generously and roll the meat in it. Melt one tablespoon of dripping and one of oil in a flameproof casserole, large enough for all the meat and vegetables, and brown the meat very thoroughly. If any flour remains, brown it, too, in a little more fat. Heat 1 pint of stock or water and pour on to the meat. Add a further ½ pint for more gravy. When gently simmering, cover and transfer to a very low oven, Reg 1/140°. After one hour put the cleaned onions and carrots on top of the meat. Half an hour later add the mushrooms. Depending on the quality of the meat, two hours should be enough to cook this stew, but longer won't hurt.

Parsley dumplings (page 53) added 20 minutes before eating the stew are a very pretty alternative to potatoes.

This stew tastes really rich, especially if proper beef stock is used. The gravy should be smooth and velvety and a good colour.

BEEF OLIVES

1 lb topside or rump steak, sliced thin
3 oz breadcrumbs
1 dessertspoon parsley, chopped
1 oz suet, finely chopped
2 anchovies, chopped
1 teaspoon lemon juice
1 egg
salt and freshly ground pepper
1 oz dripping
1 oz flour
1 pint fresh stock or water

Beat the beef to flatten it. Cut into pieces about 3 x 1½ inches. Make a stuffing with the breadcrumbs, parsley, suet, anchovies, lemon juice, beaten egg, salt and pepper. Lay a little of this on each strip of beef, roll up and tie with a piece of string. Heat the dripping in a frying pan and brown the beef rolls all over. Remove and drain on kitchen paper, while you sprinkle the flour into the pan, brown it, then add hot water or stock gradually, stirring to avoid lumps. Bring to the boil, season, return the meat and simmer uncovered for one hour, turning the rolls occasionally. When tender remove the string or thread from the olives and put them with the gravy into a hot dish.

For 4

BEEF GOULASH

2 lbs stewing beef, leg or chuck
2 lbs onions
1 lb tomatoes, skinned and quartered
2 dessertspoons paprika
8 peppercorns
salt
dripping

Trim the beef carefully and cut into cubes. Peel and quarter the onions, or cut into eights if very large. Fry them in two tablespoons of dripping in a flameproof casserole, put them aside and brown the beef, adding more dripping if necessary. Return the onions, sprinkle with paprika and stir in well. Add the tomatoes, peppercorns and salt to taste. Cover and put in a low oven, Reg 2/150°, for two hours or until tender.

This is very good reheated the following day. The juice from the tomatoes and from the meat and onions, which is extracted with the help of the paprika, provides an astounding amount of delicious thick gravy.

Serve with plain boiled potatoes, on to which you can sprinkle some dill seeds if liked.

For 4

CHILLI CON CARNE

2 lbs beef, skirt or chuck
1 lb red kidney beans
2 large onions, chopped
olive oil
2 teaspoons ground turmeric
1 tablespoon ground coriander
1–2 teaspoons ground chillt
teaspoon fresh green chilli, chopped
2 cloves garlic, crushed
1 lb tomatoes, peeled and chopped
salt and freshly ground pepper

Soak the beans overnight. Fry the chopped onions in olive oil in a flameproof casserole, turn up the heat and add the meat cut in one-inch cubes. Fry fairly fast for 5–10 minutes, scraping the sediment from the bottom of the casserole. Add the spices, garlic and chilli and continue to fry, stirring, for several minutes. Then add the peeled chopped tomatoes, salt and pepper and simmer, covered, for about two hours until the meat is tender. Meanwhile the beans should be put in a large pan of cold water and brought slowly to the boil; add salt after one hour. They take 1½–2 hours to cook and can be combined with the meat half an hour before serving, or served separately. A dish of plain white rice is a good foil to the dark beans and hot beef stew.

For 6–8

POT-AU-FEU

3 lbs topside of beef
1 clove garlic
2 oz lard or back pork fat
1 lb beef marrow bones, broken up
small tablespoon salt
6 carrots, peeled
3 turnips, peeled
1 parsnip, peeled
1 large onion, stuck with cloves
4 leeks, 1 stick celery
small bunch parsley
slices of French bread

Put the beef, stuck with slivers of garlic for flavour, and little pieces of lard which keep it moist, into four or five pints of cold water. Add the bones and bring to the boil. Turn down the heat at once; skim and keep skimming until no more scum rises, and then add the salt and vegetables, the leeks, celery and parsley tied in a bundle.

When the liquid comes to the boil again, turn the heat very low, so the liquid is just moving or trembling and simmer four or five hours. Throw out the bones. Take out the beef and vegetables and keep them hot. Let the liquid stand for five minutes, and skim off all the fat. Now put a scalded fine cloth in a wire sieve, over a bowl and strain the liquid through this. Taste for seasoning and put to keep hot. Put some pieces of French bread, previously toasted, on a plate, sprinkle them with some of the fat from the top of the soup, heat them under the grill and serve these with the soup. Serve the beef and vegetables as a second course with some sea salt crystals to hand round, or aioli (page 136) or horseradish (page 138).

The French often sieve the vegetables and serve them as a purée. They do become pretty soggy, so add fresh ones about one hour before the end, and boil some potatoes to serve with the beef.

The most important thing about a pot-au-feu *is that it should be cooked very, very slowly once the broth has been skimmed and the vegetables added.*

For 6

OXTAIL STEW

2 small or 1 very large oxtail, jointed
dripping, or butter and oil for browning
seasoned flour
4 oz salt pork or bacon, cut in cubes
glass red wine (optional)
2–3 large onions, peeled and stuck with cloves
2 cloves garlic, bouquet garni
2 tablespoons or 1 small tin tomato purée
1 pint beef stock, water or bouillon
1 lb carrots, 1 turnip, 1 lb leeks
4–5 sticks celery, seasoning

Start early in the morning by soaking the pieces of oxtail in cold salt water, for 2–4 hours. Remove and dry them well. Prepare the vegetables, cutting up everything but the leeks. Preheat the oven to Reg 2/150°. Roll the pieces of meat in four or five tablespoons of well-seasoned flour until they are thoroughly coated. Heat the dripping or butter and oil in a large flameproof casserole and toss the bacon or pork cubes in it until the fat starts to run. Remove them, and brown the oxtail pieces very well all over. Pour in the wine and let it bubble up, then add the pork, onions, garlic, herbs, half the carrots, the turnip and the warmed water or stock mixed with the tomato puree. Bring slowly to the boil and put the casserole, covered, into the oven. Cook at Reg 2/150° for one hour, then at Reg 1½/140° for a further 2–3 hours.

Three quarters of an hour before serving skim the fat off the top of the stew, check the seasoning and add the remaining vegetables. Continue cooking until they are tender. Skim again before serving with potatoes and/or dumplings (page 53).

This is not a traditional English oxtail stew and has a richer flavour.

For 4–6

CORNED BEEF HASH

8 oz tin of corned beef, cut into chunks
1 lb potatoes, peeled, boiled and cut in cubes
4 onions, sliced and fried golden in lard
lard or dripping
salt, freshly ground pepper, and a dash of Worcester sauce

Mix all the ingredients together with a fork, in a large bowl. Heat a couple of tablespoons of lard or dripping in the biggest frying pan you have. Tip the hash into the hot fat and flatten it gently. Cook for about five minutes, shaking the pan from time to time. When a crust has formed over the bottom of the hash put a large flat plate over the frying pan and turn the whole thing over. Put another tablespoon of lard or dripping in the now empty frying pan. Slide the hash back into the pan with the crust now on top. Cook another five minutes, until there is a rustling crust on the bottom.

Serve in big slices; it should be lovely and moist inside. It will keep warm in a low oven for a while without going soggy.

For 4

STEAK AND KIDNEY PUDDING

For the pudding:

8 oz self-raising flour
4 oz shredded beef suet
salt
water
For the filling.
1 lb decent stewing steak
3 lambs kidneys or 4–6 oz ox kidney
2 oz seasoned flour
stock
1 medium-sized onion, chopped
½ lb mushrooms, sliced (if liked)

Trim the meat and cut it into neat pieces. Skin, core, and slice the kidneys. Roll meat and kidney in seasoned flour. Add onion and mushrooms (if liked). Make the pastry by mixing suet, flour and salt with a little cold water. Roll it out and, keeping a piece for the lid, line a greased pudding basin.

(This basin should be large enough for the pudding to increase in size a little during cooking.) Put in the meat, etc., adding a little more seasoning and cold stock almost to cover. Shape the lid, damp the edges of the pastry, and seal firmly. The pudding should be at least one inch below the top of the basin. Cover with greased paper, then foil, or a cloth, and tie well (see page 205). Cook in a large pan of boiling water (with a lid) for 5 hours. Keep the water boiling and well topped up. You can cook it half one day and half the next if necessary. Serve it turned out of the basin with more gravy and plain boiled potatoes, carrots or cabbage, and mustard.

Some people prefer to leave out the onions and mushrooms. Cook it less long if you use better quality meat.

For 4–6

HAMBURGERS

1–2 slices home-made type bread
1 lb minced beef
1 small onion, chopped
1 clove garlic, finely chopped
parsley, thyme, pinch nutmeg
salt and freshly ground pepper
oil and butter for frying

Soak the bread in water, squeeze dry and crumble into a bowl. Add the meat, onions, garlic, herbs and seasoning and mix thoroughly. Shape into 12 small, flat round cakes on a floured board.

Heat oil and butter in a large frying pan over a moderate heat and fry the hamburgers for three or four minutes on each side, depending on how well you like them cooked. They can be pink and juicy inside, or brown right through. Serve with fried onions, or plain, or with fresh tomato sauce (page 143). They are much cheaper than frozen ones, a good deal less than half the price, and they taste better.

For 4

POOR MAN'S CASSOULET

2½ lbs meaty end of fresh belly of pork
1 lb dried haricot beans, soaked overnight
1 onion, peeled
1 lb tomatoes, skinned and chopped
1 clove garlic, crushed
salt and freshly ground pepper

The pork belly should be boned and cut in one-inch slices. Roast these slices in a medium hot oven, Reg 5/190°, for 15 minutes. Put the beans in a pan with the onion and cover by an inch with cold water. Bring to the boil and simmer 45 minutes. Put the tomatoes in a casserole with the lightly roasted pork and its juices, the crushed clove of garlic, the beans, onion and half the liquid in which they were cooked. Add salt and pepper and cook in a low oven, Reg 3/160°, for two hours, keeping closely covered. This is better if made the day before and reheated. The juice should be rich and creamy.

For 6

PORK KEBABS

2 lbs leg of pork, off the bone
oregano
fresh lemon juice
freshly ground pepper
olive oil
salt

Even in the cheapest Greek restaurants they do use leg of pork rather than a cheaper cut, because it is so much better.

Cut the pork into little cubes and sprinkle liberally with oregano, lemon juice and pepper. Allow it to soak up these flavours for a couple of hours, turning the cubes over from time to time. Thread the cubes on skewers and shake off as much lemon juice as you can. Brush with oil and grill fast for five minutes, turning frequently. Sprinkle with salt and pepper and eat with a salad of green bottled chillies, lettuce and raw onions, and with plain rice. The bottled chillies can be found at most continental provision stores and delicatessens.

For 4–6

FRIED PORK FILLET

1 small pork fillet
juice of ½ lemon
salt and freshly ground pepper
butter for frying

Slice the pork into little rounds about ¼ inch thick. There will seem a lot, but they shrink in cooking. Between two pieces of greaseproof paper beat the little rounds of meat flat with a rolling pin. Season with lemon juice, plenty of fresh ground black pepper and a little salt. Melt the butter in a frying pan, and when it starts to brown slide in half the little escalopes of pork. As soon as the edges become whitish, flip the pieces over. They should fry quite quickly and be delicately browned and juicy after three or four minutes on each side. Slide on to a hot dish and fry the remaining pieces. When they are done and removed to the hot dish, squeeze any remaining lemon juice into the pan and add a little hot water (sherry is good too if you have it). Pour the pan juices over the meat and eat with a carefully made puree of creamy potatoes. These little escalopes are just as good in flavour as veal and much juicier.

Pork fillet is also called pork tenderloin. It is a totally lean piece of meat, and a good buy because there is no waste at all.

For 2

STUFFED PORK FILLET

1 small pork fillet (tenderloin)
1 small Italian, or other spicy sausage
2 oz mushrooms, chopped and sweated in butter
1 beaten egg yolk
parsley, chopped
salt and freshly ground pepper
2 rashers streaky bacon
butter for roasting

Preheat oven to Reg 5/190°. Score the fillet down the middle twice, lengthwise, taking care not to cut right through. You can now flatten it out like an oblong piece of pastry; bang it even flatter with a rolling pin.

Skin the sausage and mix the contents in a bowl with the egg yolk, chopped mushrooms, sweated in butter, chopped parsley and seasoning. Put this stuffing in a line down the middle of the flattened fillet. Fold the fillet over the stuffing and fasten into a long sausage shape with string or toothpicks. Cover the joint, which should be pressed together well, with the bacon slices, rinds removed, to keep the meat moist (see diagram opposite).

Cover with foil and repast with a little butter at Reg 5/190°, for 40–45 minutes, removing the foil for the last ten minutes. Remove the string or toothpicks and cut the meat into little round slices, each prettily enclosing a nugget of stuffing, and serve with a thin gravy made with the pan juices and a little dry white wine or cider. The fillet can be dry if overcooked, but always tastes very delicious.

For 2–3

SALT PORK

If you buy salt pork at a supermarket, you can be sure it will not be over-salty, because they are consistent about the amount of time the meat stays in the brine. However, many small butchers keep pieces of meat in the brine-tub indefinitely to preserve them; it is essential to find out, when buying from a butcher with a vast brine-tub, just how long each piece of pork has been there, how salty it is, and how long a soaking it will need. Do not be put off by the butcher's suggestion of bringing the meat to the boil in a pan of water and then throwing this water away. This does not work on very salty pork; it does need soaking, overnight at least.

SALT PORK WITH PEAS

2 lbs salt pork belly (lean end), skin removed
1 large onion, sliced
6 carrots, sliced lengthwise
2 bay leaves
bunch of parsley and thyme, tied with a thread
8 oz yellow split peas
salt if needed

Soak the pork, overnight if necessary. Put it in a large saucepan, cover with cold water and bring to the boil. In the meantime prepare the vegetables. Add them and the herbs to the pork and simmer for two hours, covered. Remove the vegetables and add the split peas to the water; taste for salt and simmer until the peas are cooked, about one hour. Some people put the peas in a cloth bag and hang it over the side of the pan in the water to cook. It does prevent them from dissolving into a mush. If they do disintegrate, strain off the liquid before serving the peas on a dish round the piece of pork.

This is a filling peasant dish.

For 6

PORK, BEEF OR CHICKEN KORMA

1½ lbs pork or beef cut into squares, or 2 lbs raw chicken joints
for the marinade:
1 teaspoon ground turmeric
1 clove garlic, crushed
1 5-oz carton plain yoghurt
1 clove garlic, 1 onion
butter for frying, salt
5 whole cloves
5 whole cardamoms
1 cinnamon stick of about 1 inch

Marinate the meat in the yoghurt, mixed with turmeric and a crushed clove of garlic, for an hour or more. Slice the onion and the whole clove of garlic and fry lightly in butter in a flameproof casserole without browning. Add the spices, fry a few minutes longer, than add the meat and its marinade. Season with a little salt.

Cook covered in a slow oven, Reg 2/150°, for 1½ hours for chicken or pork, two hours for beef.

This curry is absolutely not hot, but is mild and spicy and very delicious contrasted with a hot one.

For 4–6

GRATIN OF HAM AND POTATOES

½ large onion, chopped
1 clove garlic, crushed and chopped
nut of butter
1 tablespoon oil
4 oz slice ham
2 eggs
½ pint milk
2 oz Gruyere, grated
1 oz Parmesan, grated
salt, freshly ground pepper and nutmeg
1 lb potatoes

Preheat oven to Reg 5/190°. Heat a little butter and the olive oil in a small frying pan and soften the onion and garlic for 10–15 minutes without browning. Add the ham cut into sticks like large matches, heat through and keep warm.

Meanwhile beat the eggs into the milk, and add the grated cheese, salt, pepper and a touch of nutmeg. Peel the potatoes and grate them coarsely; squeeze out the water with your hands (there will be more than you think). Mix the whole lot together in a bowl, turn it into a buttered oval gratin dish, and dot the top with butter. Bake in the top of the oven for 30–35 minutes; finish off by browning under the grill.

This is a very good lunch for a winter's day.

For 4

ROAST BEST END OF LAMB

A best end usually consists of six or seven chops joined together, so one is enough for three people. Get the butcher to chop and chine it, and to tear off the tough skin.

Preheat the oven to Reg 3/160°. Rub the fat with a mixture of oil and lemon juice, or oil and salt, and insert slivers of^arlic and rosemary here and there. Roast at Reg 3/160° for about one hour or at Reg 5/190° for 45 minutes. Make a gravy from the pan juices and stock or white wine. Carve the meat into juicy, pink little chops, and serve with Pommes Rissolées (page 126).

For 3

SHOULDER OF LAMB WITH AVGOLEMONO SAUCE

1 shoulder lamb
4 cloves garlic
2 lbs broad beans
2 egg yolks
juice 1 lemon
salt and pepper
a little chicken stock
butter or oil for roasting

Ask the butcher to chop the shoulder down through the bone, but not right through the meat underneath, to make slices one inch thick. The shoulder is now easy to carve into slices but still in one piece (see diagram). Put in a roasting pan, fat side up, with the peeled cloves of garlic in the cuts. Spread the joint with a little butter or oil, sprinkle with salt and pepper, and roast at Reg 5/190° for ¾–1 hour, basting two or three times.

Meanwhile cook the shelled broad beans in boiling salted water and drain, keeping some of the water they cooked in. Beat together the egg yolks and lemon juice and add about half a cup of the bean liquid. When the lamb is cooked remove it from the roasting pan and keep it warm on a dish in the oven. Remove the garlic and skim off the fat from the juices in the pan, before stirring them into the egg and lemon sauce. Put this sauce in a pan over a very low flame, add the broad beans and about two tablespoons of stock, season and thicken very gently – it takes a long time – without ever boiling.

Slice up the shoulder, pour on the sauce, and serve with plain rice or baked potatoes and a simple salad.

This is a Greek dish and very delicious; the lemon counteracts the richness of a fat shoulder very well.

For 6

EPIGRAMS OF LAMB

1 lb breast of lamb
1½ oz butter, melted
1 egg, beaten
pinch thyme
1 cupful fresh white breadcrumbs
salt and freshly ground pepper
Béarnaise sauce (page 141), or tomato sauce (page 143)

Remove the bones, gristle and some of the fat from the cooked lamb while it is still warm, and cut into neat fingers or squares when cold. Mix the melted butter with the beaten egg, thyme and seasoning. Dip each piece of lamb into this mixture, then into fresh breadcrumbs.

Grill under a moderate heat until browned both sides, and serve with Bearnaise or tomato sauce. They make crisp little morsels which should be enjoyed by children.

This dish is quite luxurious and rich, and yet is made out of the most humble piece of meat that has already done a stint in the cooking of Scotch Broth (see page 14). It is definitely better if it is eaten fairly soon after it comes out of the broth.

For 2–3

BOILED LEG OF LAMB AND CAPER SAUCE

1 large leg New Zealand lamb
1 swede orturnip
1 leek, 1 onion, 2 carrots
2 tablespoons sea salt, less if using ordinary salt
for caper sauce:
salt
1 oz butter, ½oz flour
3 or 4 tablespoons lamb cooking liquid
1 tablespoon capers
1 tablespoon caper vinegar
single cream

Cover the leg of lamb with cold water in a large saucepan, and bring it slowly to the boil. Skim impeccably, add the peeled whole vegetables and salt. Simmer, covered, very slowly so the water just turns lazily in the pan, and keep skimmed. It will take 1¾–2 hours. Strain well before serving. Make a sauce with the butter, flour, three to four tablespoons of lamb broth, strained, and the caper vinegar. Add the capers and a little cream, and the onion that cooked with the lamb, chopped fairly small. Season the sauce and serve in a jug: it should be the consistency of cream. Serve with boiled potatoes.

For 6–8

IRISH STEW

3 lbs neck of lamb
3 lbs smallish potatoes
1 lb onions, sliced
½ lb carrots, peeled and sliced
2 leeks, cut in one-inch pieces
1 young turnip, peeled and sliced
plenty of salt and freshly ground pepper
parsley, chopped

The usual Irish stew is a very basic dish. If, however, you put whole potatoes on top of your stew, they absorb the fat, making them delicious. A wide shallow casserole is better than a deep narrow one, so that the fat can reach all the potatoes.

Peel the potatoes, and cut half of them into thin slices and place in the bottom of a buttered casserole. Put the prepared vegetables on top of them, season and then add the lamb, cut in chops and with all the accessible fat removed. Season again and cover with whole potatoes. Sprinkle with quarter of a pint of water or stock, and put a piece of oiled greaseproof paper over the potatoes. Cover with a tight-fitting lid and bake at Reg 3/160° for 2½ hours. Remove the greaseproof paper. Sprinkle the top with parsley before serving.

For 6–8

LAMB POLO

1 lb dried apricots
2 boned shoulders lamb
4 onions, chopped
4 oz butter (2 oz are for the rice)
2 teaspoons ground coriander
1 teaspoon ground cinnamon
2 teaspoons ground cumin
salt and freshly ground pepper
2 lbs rice

Pour one pint of boiling water over the apricots and allow them to soak for an hour or two. Start cooking the rice in the Persian way (page 166). Trim most of the fat from the meat, and cut it into one-inch squares.

Melt half the butter in a large flameproof casserole, soften the chopped onions and brown lightly, stirring all the time. Turn up the heat and add the lamb. Brown all over very thoroughly and add the spices. Fry them, stirring well, for two or three minutes, then add the apricots with the water in which they soaked, plenty of salt and plenty of pepper. Add enough water just to cover the meat and simmer, covered, for 1½ hours, or until tender, stirring from time to time. Serve with Persian rice.

This beautiful, spicy Persian recipe is improved by being kept and reheated.

For 10–12

LANCASHIRE HOT-POT

2–3 lbs middle neck of lamb, cut into chops and trimmed of fat
8 medium potatoes, peeled and thickly sliced
3 medium onions, sliced
3 lambs' kidneys, skinned, cored and sliced
4 oz mushrooms, sliced if large
12 shelled oysters are traditional but not vital
1 oz dripping
1 oz flour
¾ pint water
salt and freshly ground pepper
½ oz butter

Preheat the oven to Reg 3/160°. Make the hot-pot in a tall round pot, of iron or earthenware. Use half the butter to grease the inside of the pot, put in half the sliced potatoes, and season them. Brown the chops in some hot dripping in a frying pan, and lay them over the potatoes. Season, and cover with a layer of onions also fried in dripping, followed by the kidneys, mushrooms, and oysters if you have them, seasoning each layer. Finish with a layer of overlapping slices of potato.

Fry the flour in the frying pan with a little more dripping, and gradually add f pint boiling water, stirring to remove the sediment from the bottom of the frying pan. Cook a few minutes to thicken a little and strain over the contents of the pot. Season the top layer, dot with butter and cover. Cook, covered, for two hours, and for a further ½ hour uncovered to brown the top.

Serve very hot with pickled red cabbage, its traditional accompaniment.

For 6

MOUSSAKA

1½ lbs cooked lamb or beef, finely chopped or minced
3 large onions, sliced
1 lb aubergines
olive oil for cooking
½ pint stock, bouillon or gravy
3 tablespoons tomato puree
salt and freshly ground pepper
for the top:
3 or 4 egg yolks
½–1 pint seasoned milk

Make the top first, as it takes up to an hour to cook; it combines so well with the aubergine flavour that it is worth making this top rather than the alternative Bechamel sauce (see page 137) .

Combine the beaten egg yolks and seasoned milk and put to thicken in the top of a double boiler, or bain-marie; don't let the water boil or the sauce will curdle. Stir with a wooden spoon from time to time, while you prepare the other ingredients. When it is like thick custard let it cool and thicken even further.

Preheat the oven to Reg 4/180°. Meanwhile slice the unpeeled aubergines thickly on the slant and fry them gently in plenty of olive oil; they should be just transparent, not browned. As they cook, lift them out and line the bottom of a deep oval casserole with some of them.

Fry the onions in more oil until brown . Put half the minced meat into the casserole on top of the aubergines, then the onions then more aubergines and the rest of the meat. Press firmly down. Mix the tomato puree and seasoning into the heated stock and pour over the meat. Spoon the custard-like top over all and cook for about one hour at Reg 4/180°.

For 5–6

GREEK MEATBALLS

1 lb fresh minced beef and lamb, mixed
2 eggs
1 clove garlic, crushed
1 medium onion, finely chopped
handful coriander leaves or parsley, chopped
½ teaspoon cinnamon
1 teaspoon salt and plenty of freshly ground pepper
3-inch piece stale French bread, or thick slice any home-made type white bread
butter and oil for frying
milk or water

Put the meat, eggs, garlic, onion, herbs and seasonings in a bowl, and mix. Soften the bread, crusts removed, in milk or water. Squeeze dry and crumble into the mixture. Mix again thoroughly – with your hands is the easiest way. On a floured board roll into walnut sized balls and fry in a mixture of butter and oil for five to six minutes, turning frequently. Serve with a fresh tomato sauce (page 143).

For 4–5

SHEPHERD'S PIE

1½ lbs minced beef, or lamb (fresh or left-over)
1 large onion
1 clove garlic
2 tomatoes
2 carrots
stock, water, parsley, bayleaf, thyme
tablespoon tomato puree
1½ lbs potatoes
¼ pint milk, 1½ oz butter
salt ancf pepper
olive oil, or dripping
dessertspoon flour, ½oz butter, for thickening

Put three or four tablespoons olive oil or dripping in a wide shallow pan and heat gently. Chop the onion and garlic finely and add them. While they are frying, peel the tomatoes and chop them finely. When the onions start to brown, add the tomatoes and cook fast, stirring, until all the water has evaporated and the sauce starts to brown. Now add the meat and carrots, grated on the coarse side of the grater. Fry fast for ten minutes more, if using raw meat, turning the meat over often.

If using left-over (cooked) meat, warm through gently. Now add half-stock, half-water to come almost to the top of the meat, but not to cover it. Add thyme, salt and pepper, bayleaf, tomato puree and a handful of chopped parsley. Left-over meat needs no further cooking, but if using fresh meat, simmer for an hour and a half, adding more stock as needed and stirring from time to time. Work a dessertspoon of plain flour into a nut of butter (about half an ounce) and drop little pieces of this paste into the mince, stirring, to thicken it. If you thicken it at the beginning it tends to separate and your mince has a lot of Spanish looking tomato-coloured oil on top. After adding the flour, cook oil for 20 minutes. Put the meat into a pie dish. Cover with creamy mashed potatoes made exactly as on page 127. Bake in a moderate oven, Reg 5/190°, for 25 minutes until nicely brown and tempting.

For 6

BLANQUETTE DE VEAU

2 lbs shoulder or breast of veal
2 bayleaves
12 peppercorns
2 onions, 4 carrots
salt
4 tablespoons good stock (if available)
2 oz butter
1 oz flour
½ lb mushrooms (optional)
2 egg yolks
1 smail lemon
4 tablespoons cream

Cut the veal into one-inch squares, removing the fat. Put in a saucepan, cover with cold water, bring to the boil and let it simmer with two bayleaves and a few peppercorns for ¾ hour. Now add the sliced onions, a piece of lemon peel, a few carrots and some salt. Four tablespoons of good stock can also be added at this stage. Simmer on for another 1½ hours. Melt the butter in another pan, stir in the flour and one pint of the hot veal broth, strained. Add the cleaned mushrooms and cook for ten minutes. Then, off the heat, add the strained pieces of veal, the egg yolks beaten with the juice of a small lemon, a little more stock if needed and the cream. Heat thoroughly, letting the egg yolks thicken slightly, taste for seasoning and serve with a fresh-looking vegetable such as French beans or fresh peas.

For 6

OX-TONGUE

1 ox-tongue, salted and if possible smoked, of about 3 lbs
3 carrots
3 onions
1 stick celery
1 fresh pig's trotter (if salted, soak with the tongue)
parsley, thyme, bayleaf, peppercorns
mustard sauce (page 139)

Soak the tongue for 24 hours changing the water once or twice. Put it in a large casserole with the sliced vegetables, add the pig's foot and enough water to cover. Throw in the peppercorns and the bunch of herbs, bring gently to the boil and simmer in the oven in a covered casserole at Reg 2/150° for 3½–4½ hours. Take out of the liquid and skin while the tongue is still very hot. Put it on a dish and serve hot with mustard sauce.

If you want it cold, strain and reduce the liquid in which it cooked to about one third, so it will set to a firm jelly when cold. Taste it for salt; if it is too salty you must dilute it and add aspic. Some cooks prefer to lay the tongue out on a plate, top side up, and glaze with the almost-set jelly, but you can roll it up, squeeze it into a straight-sided round dish, fill the spaces with the reduced cooking liquid, press with a weighted plate for 24 hours, and turn it out before serving. Some people think it looks prettier like this in a jellied shape, and that laid out on a dish it looks as though it will say "ouch" when you cut it.

For 6

CALVES' TONGUES WITH SALT PORK

¾ lb salt pork belly (lean end, not soaked)
4 calves' tongues
1 onion
1 stick celery
2 carrots
sprigs parsley
peppercorns

Put the cleaned chopped vegetables in a large saucepan with the parsley and peppercorns, tongues and freshly salted pork, rind removed. Just cover with water, bring to the boil and simmer really slowly for 2¼–2½ hours, with the water just moving gently. The salt from the pork is absorbed by the tongues as they cook.

When they are tender take them out and skin them, as soon as they are cool enough, starting underneath the tips and removing the skin from front to back in large pieces. Remove any bones, trim them, and put into a hot dish with the salt pork, removed from the bone and cut into large cubes (about two inches across). Sprinkle with chopped parsley and serve very hot with parsley sauce or mustard sauce (page 139) and plain boiled potatoes.

For 4

PIGS' KIDNEYS WITH LOVAGE

2 pigs' kidneys
salt and freshly ground pepper
pork dripping, or oil and butter
juice of ½ lemon
1 tablespoon lovage, finely chopped, or celery leaves or celery salt

About half an hour before you will eat them, slice the kidneys finely, removing all the fatty core, and sprinkle with salt and pepper. Leave for 25 minutes. Melt the fat, or oil and butter, in a thick frying pan, so that the bottom is liberally covered. Raise the heat and fry the kidney slices briskly, a few at a time, so that each slice gets an even contact with the heat. As soon as both sides have changed colour from dark red to pale brown, put the pieces in a heated serving dish.

Finish by sprinkling with lemon juice and chopped lovage. Serve at once with their own juices and mashed potato.

Lovage, once you have it, is very easy to grow and is perennial like mint. It is similar in flavour to raw celery leaves; if you haven't any lovage use celery instead.

For 2

KEBABS WITH LAMBS' KIDNEYS

4 lambs' kidneys
4 rashers bacon, rinds removed
1 large onion
6 firm tomatoes
1 pimento, seeds removed
12 small mushrooms
12 basil leaves
juice of ½ lemon
olive oil
salt and freshly ground pepper
2 bayleaves
thyme

Skin, core and slice each kidney into four pieces. Cut the bacon into one-inch squares. Quarter the onions and part the pieces, halve the tomatoes, cut the pimento into one-inch squares, remove the mushroom stalks.

Put the meat and vegetables, including the basil leaves, in a bowl, and sprinkle with lemon juice, plenty of olive oil, salt, pepper and thyme. Add the bayleaves and marinate for about half an hour.

Divide everything between eight skewers, alternating the ingredients and putting the basil leaves against the cut side of the tomatoes.

Grill or barbecue, brushing with more oil, turning frequently. They take five or ten minutes. Serve with plain rice and a green salad. Mix the left-over marinade (and the juices from the grill-pan if you are indoors) into the rice before serving.

For 4

KIDNEYS WITH LEMON JUICE

4 lambs' kidneys, skinned and cored
3 cloves garlic
juice of ½ lemon
dash white wine
salt and freshly ground pepper
sprig parsley, chopped
oil for frying

Chop the kidneys into pieces about ¾ inch thick. Heat a heavy frying pan until it is very very hot. Chop the garlic and when the pan is ready pour in a little oil, just enough to cover the bottom, and throw in the garlic. To this add the kidneys and sauté them three or four minutes, moving and turning them with a wooden spoon or fork all the time. Add the lemon juice, wine, chopped parsley and seasoning. Let it sizzle up and serve immediately with rice.

For 2

KIDNEY PILAFF

5 lambs' kidneys
1 onion, sliced
1 tablespoon olive oil
1 tablespoon butter
2 bayleaves
sprig of thyme
2 tablespoons tomato purée, moistened with a little stock
salt and freshly ground pepper
1 dessertspoon wine vinegar

Sauté the onion in oil and butter without browning. Skin and core the kidneys and chop them into thin slices. Sauté with the onions, bayleaves and thyme, for five to six minutes. Add the tomato purée and stock, and the vinegar, salt and pepper. Stir in and heat through. Serve with plain rice.

For 2

ROGNON DE BOEUF SAIGNANT

1 ox kidney
2½ oz unsalted butter
small bunch parsley
salt and freshly ground pepper

Cut the kidney into half-inch slices, removing the core. Chop the parsley. Heat one ounce of the butter in a heavy frying pan. When it is really hot, with a blue haze rising, put in the slices of kidney. Saute for two or three minutes, moving them around in the pan. Turn them over and cook the other side in the same way. Meanwhile melt the rest of the butter in a small pan with the chopped parsley, without letting it brown. When the slices of kidney are browned on both sides, put them in a heated dish, throwing out the butter in which they cooked. Pour the freshly melted butter and parsley over, sprinkle with salt and freshly ground pepper and serve immediately. They will be very pink inside and very tasty; the red juice which they make mingles well with the butter. Serve with watercress and pureed potatoes.

For 4

GRILLED LIVER ON A SKEWER

¾ lb liver, lambs' or calves', sliced thickly
1 onion
1 red or green pimento
2 tablespoons olive oil
juice of ½ lemon
thyme
salt and freshly ground pepper

Prepare one hour before you start to cook. Cut the liver into squares about § inch across. Cut the onions and pimentoes into pieces about the same size. Mix the olive oil and lemon juice, salt, pepper and thyme. Marinate the liver, peppers and onions in this for an hour.

Take out the pieces of meat and vegetables and put them.on skewers, alternating meat, onion and pepper. Grill under a fairly fast heat, turning from time to time. Serve with plain boiled rice, to which you can add the juices from the grill pan.

For 2–3

LIVER PROVENÇALE

1 lb lambs' liver, cut in thin slices
olive oil
2 cloves garlic
small bunch parsley
flour
butter
wine vinegar
salt and freshly ground pepper

Chop the garlic and parsley finely. Pat a little flour, seasoned with salt and pepper, into the liver to absorb the moisture. Heat half a tablespoon of oil in a really heavy frying pan. Meanwhile in a saucepan melt a good dollop of butter, without browning, and add the chopped garlic and parsley.

When the oil is really hot, with a blue haze rising, put in the slices of liver, flip them over and remove them to a hot dish. They should not have more than one or two minutes' cooking altogether. Take the frying pan off the heat and add the butter and garlic mixture. Add a dash of vinegar, let it sizzle up and pour it, still sizzling, over the liver.

Serve immediately with a purée of potatoes or turnips.

For 4

SWEETBREADS

To prepare any sweetbread, whatever the recipe, start by washing under a running tap, or soak in frequently changed salted water for one to three hours, until they are no longer pink but pearly white. Put into a pan of cold, salted water and bring slowly to the boil; boil two or three minutes, remove and cool at once in cold water. This stiffens them, making them easier to handle. Skin and remove all the lumps of gristle you can. Press between two plates for an hour.

The main methods of cooking from this point are: Poaching – poach in stock until tender, then use in a fricassee. Frying – (1) slice the sweetbreads; flour, egg-and-crumb and fry gently. Serve with tomato sauce (page 143); (2) slice, dip in fritter batter and fry gently; (3) slice and sauté in butter, for 10–15 minutes. After they are cooked, make a quick sauce in the pan with cream and a few mushrooms previously sautéed in butter, or serve them plain, sprinkled with lemon juice.

FRICASSEED SWEETBREADS

1 lb poached sweetbreads, kept warm
1 pint of stock in which they were poached
1 oz butter
1 oz flour
juice of 1 lemon
2 egg yolks
salt and freshly ground pepper
parsley, chopped
½ lb mushrooms (optional)

Strain one pint of the stock in which the sweetbreads were poached and make a sauce with the flour and butter and strained liquid. Mix the lemon juice with the egg yolks, season with salt and pepper and add to the sauce, away from the heat, stirring attentively; once it is mixed in, the sauce can no longer curdle. Let it thicken, then pour the sauce over the sliced sweetbreads and sprinkle with parsley. Serve with boiled or mashed potatoes.

You can add ½ lb mushrooms, first cooked in the stock, to the sauce.

For 4

SAUSAGE MEAT

¾ lb cheap cut of pork
4 lb pork fat
2 thickish slices bread (about 3 oz)
grated rind lemon
pinch nutmeg
2 teaspoons salt
1 teaspoon freshly ground pepper
parsley, sage and thyme, finely chopped
touch of garlic if liked

Trim the meat. Soak the bread in water, squeeze dry and crumble into a large bowl. Mince the meat once, then add the fat and mince again, not too finely. Put into the bowl with the bread and add the lemon peel, herbs, spices and seasoning. Mix thoroughly with your hands. If you can get sausage skins, rinse them through under the cold tap, and then fill them. If you haven't an electric mincer with a sausage-filling attachment, run the skin on to a large funnel and push the meat through with the handle of a wooden spoon. Twist at intervals to make separate sausages. If you cannot buy sausage skins, make skinless sausages rolled in flour.

It makes about 16 medium sausages.

SAUSAGES WITH WHITE WINE SAUCE

1½ lbs spicy French or Italian sausages
glass white wine
1½ oz butter
1 oz flour
½ pint milk (infused with onion, bayleaf and peppercorns)
salt and freshly ground pepper
mashed potatoes o/'cooked haricot beans

Make half a pint of Bechamel with one ounce of butter, and the flour and milk (see page 137). Season with salt and pepper. Soak the sausages in lukewarm water for a few minutes – this helps to prevent them from bursting. Dry them, prick all over and fry gently in the remaining half ounce of butter until practically done, pouring the fat off from time to time. Add the wine, and when it is reduced by half, take out the sausages and keep hot, or.arrange them on a mountain of mashed potatoes, or plain, cooked haricot beans. Add the Bechamel to the wine in the frying pan, stir it well and pour over the sausages. This sauce is a good addition to bangers and mash, but the bangers need to be a bit special to be worth it.

For 4

TOAD IN THE HOLE

6 large sausages
6 slices streaky bacon
for the batter:
4 oz plain flour
salt
2 eggs
½ pint milk
2–3 tablespoons oil or good pork dripping

Make a pudding batter by sieving the flour and salt into a bowl, make a well in the centre and add the eggs, breaking the yolks with your spoon before you start stirring. Add the milk gradually, stirring in the flour little by little until half the milk is added; keep going until all the flour is taken up and the mixture is smooth. Then add the rest of the milk and beat for five or ten minutes. Stand the batter in a cool place for one hour.

Preheat oven to Reg 9/245°. When batter is ready, skin the sausages, heat the oil or dripping in a baking tin, fry the bacon two or three minutes, then add the skinned halved sausages. Put the tin in the oven for five minutes, then pour on the batter and cook for five minutes at Reg 9/245° and 35–40 minutes at Reg 7/220°.

For 4

SAUSAGE WITH LENTILS

1 cotechino or poaching sausage, of ¾–1 lb
¾ lb small green lentils.
2 cloves garlic
1 stick celery, chopped
butter
salt

Soak the lentils for three or four hours, then wash them and place in a pan of cold water with the peeled cloves of garlic and stick of celery. Bring slowly to the boil, skim and simmer gently for 1–1½ hours, adding salt half-way through, when they have started to get tender. Three-quarters of an hour before you want it ready, put the sausage, pricked all over with a needle, into a pan of cold water.

Bring it gradually to the boil and poach in slowly simmering water for three-quarters of an hour.

Strain the lentils, keeping the liquid for soup, and add a large nut of butter. Serve with the sausage cut in slices and a good glass of rough red wine.

For 4

STUFFED VINE LEAVES

20–30 vine leaves, fresh, or bought ready for use at Greek or Cypriot shops
3 oz rice (6 oz cooked rice)
4 oz minced lamb, beef or pork, raw or cooked
1 smail onion
pinch ground coriander (or fresh leaves)
pinch ground cumin
salt and freshly ground pepper
good squeeze of lemon
¼ –½ pint stock or tomato juice
olive oil

If you have fresh vine leaves, trim off the stalks and plunge them into boiling salted water for five minutes. Drain and let them cool while you fry the onion, finely chopped, in oil until it is quite brown.

Boil the rice, unless you have some ready cooked. Brown the meat with the onions if you are using fresh meat; if using cold cooked meat, chop it finely. Mix the onion, meat, rice and spices, and add salt and pepper to taste. Put a teaspoon of the mixture on the rough side of each leaf, wrap neatly into a little parcel, lay them side by side in a flat flameproof dish (they don't need tying), squeeze lemon juice over and pour on the stock or tomato juice. Cover with a plate that fits right down on to the vine leaves, to stop them coming apart. Cook over a very low heat for half an hour. Serve cold.

These are good served with drinks before dinner, especially if you have your own vine, and can make them quite small, choosing leaves that make good wrappers – not too indented, and not too old and tough.

Makes 20–30

CHICKEN LIVERS WITH SAGE

1 lb chicken livers, cut in pieces
1 oz butter
2 slices bacon, rinds removed, cut in pieces
salt and freshly ground pepper
3 or 4 fresh sage leaves, chopped, or 1 teaspoon dried sage
sherry

Melt the butter in a small iron pan, and sauté the pieces of bacon for a minute or two. Add the chicken livers, a little salt, pepper and sage and cook five minutes, stirring them about a bit.

Remove the chicken livers and bacon to a hot dish and keep them warm, while you add a dash of sherry and a similar amount of water to the pan, and let it sizzle for a minute, stirring to release the sediment. Pour the juices over the livers and serve with Risotto Milanese (page 129) or plain boiled rice.

For 4

POULTRY & GAME

It really is worth buying boiling chickens; it may seem more difficult because of the time factor, but, thinking ahead, you can put a nice fat hen in a pot with some herbs and vegetables, cover it with water and put it to simmer very gently while you go out. It can sit there for hours, gradually becoming tender, and it makes large amounts of delicious broth. It is worth going further to find a bird that has had a happy life, but even a battery hen has a remote resemblance to chicken, once carefully cooked. All poultry is now fairly cheap, since it is reared on such a vast scale.

When you buy a fresh chicken, don't forget to take home the giblets (and if you buy a frozen one don't forget to look inside before you cook it, as polythene does not make a good stuffing); the giblets are invaluable for gravy or stock or to improve the. flavour of the sauce that goes with the chicken, and the liver is a good addition to most stuffings.

Game, both for casseroling and roasting, is getting scarcer and more expensive every year, but still seems to be cheaper in the country. It is worth remembering that the birds are only young and plump at the beginning of the season, and become increasingly thin and tough as the winter wears on. Young pigeons are available only from March to October, and even in those months make certain you have not got dad or granddad from the year before. The same applies to wild bunnies, though tame rabbits are not allowed to go on hopping about long enough to get tough.

Full instructions are given for the drawing, plucking and trussing of birds, and the drawing and skinning of rabbits or hares, for anyone lucky enough to get a present of game, but a pheasant run into by a car is unlikely to make good eating, poor thing, because of the bruises.

TRUSSING

This method does not use skewers.

Lay the drawn bird on its back with its tail towards you and make the cuts shown in the diagram; tuck the front flap of skin at its neck over the neck hole and down over the back. Flip the pinions (the last joint of the wing) inwards and tuck them behind the shoulders.

Take about 3 feet of string and pass it under the bird's shoulders, the loose ends being one in each hand on each side of the bird.

Pull the string up under the wings of the bird, over the shoulders, down the back of each wing, past the elbows, past the legs. Pull it up under the thigh joints and, without letting go, pull it all tight, and flip the bird over onto its front. Tie a knot in the middle of the back, and turn it over again.

The bird should now be looking much neater, plumped up with its legs drawn up to its wings.

Bring the two ends of the string down the back and knot them over the parson's nose. If you want to stuff the bird, do it now.

Bring the ends of the string from the knot on the parson's nose and tie the drumsticks firmly together, below the breastbone.

BONING A CHICKEN OR DUCK

Find a knife with a short thin blade and sharpen it extra well.

Turn the drawn chicken over and cut along the middle of its back from neck to tail. Sliding your knife hard up against the carcass of the bird, work your way round one side, slowly pulling the meat away with your fingers to expose the line for your next cut.

When you encounter the leg, feel with your free forefinger for the ball and socket joint and slide the point of your knife into it to free it. Continue cutting round, disengaging the wing, but cutting outside the fine flat bone that lies beneath it on the carcass. When you have cut round to the flat side of the breastbone, start on the other side of the back in the same way. Cut the skin from the ridge of the breastbone very carefully indeed as it is paper-thin here.

Lift out the carcass, leaving the parson's nose on it. You can remove the upper leg and wing bones by sliding your fingers and knife down close to the bone and cutting firmly through the joint. Remove the wing tips completely, skin, bone and all, or you can leave the last two wing bones and the drumsticks (shown as dotted outlines) where they are.

The flesh can now be flattened out, skin side down, seasoned and sprinkled with wine, and any rich stuffing put in the centre. The bird is wrapped round this and made more or less into a chicken shape again, and the opening tied, skewered or sewn together. You can roast this stuffed chicken or simmer it in stock.

A paté mixture of pork and veal with perhaps a few pistachio nuts and a good proportion of fat makes an excellent stuffing. Serve it cold, with the threads removed and the seam-side down. Cut it right across in slices like any pate. You can bone a duck in exactly the same way. If you sew the opening rather than tying it, the bird miraculously goes back into shape while it is cooking.

CHICKEN PIE

1 small boiling chicken
2 carrots, 1 onion
8 peppercorns, 1 bayleaf, salt
1 oz butter, 1 oz flour
juice of ½ lemon
chopped parsley
6 rashers bacon
4 oz mushrooms
plain pie pastry (page 172)
top of the milk

Cover the chicken with water in a large saucepan, bring slowly to the boil, skim and add the sliced vegetables, bayleaf, peppercorns and salt. Simmer for 11 hours or longer, until the bird is tender. Allow to cool a little in the cooking liquid. Preheat oven to Reg 7/220°. Make a sauce with the butter, flour and ¾ pint of the strained, hot chicken broth. Throw in the mushrooms whole and simmer for eight minutes. Check for seasoning. Skin the chicken and cut it into pieces. Roll the bacon rashers, rinds removed, and keep together with toothpicks while you fry them gently for 15 minutes. Remove the toothpicks.

Mix the chicken pieces, chopped parsley and lemon juice into two thirds of the mushroom sauce, keeping the remaining sauce aside, and turn the mixture into a pie dish. Lay the bacon rolls on top and

cover with pastry. Brush with top of the milk and bake at Reg 7/220° for ten minutes and then at Reg 4/180° for 20 minutes or longer. Serve with the extra sauce.

A bright green vegetable such as sprouts, broccoli, or best of allfresh peas, sets off the pale interior of the pie. It is also delicious eaten cold.

For 4–6

CHICKEN AND LEEKS

1 small chicken
4 small leeks
1 oz butter
4 oz long grain rice
1 pint milk
salt and freshly ground pepper

Clean the leeks and cut into one-inch pieces. Soften in the butter for five to ten minutes without letting them even start to brown. Cut the chicken into four large pieces and skin them. Leave the carcass for stock.

Butter a casserole and arrange a layer of leeks in the bottom, add two pieces of chicken, sprinkle on half the rice, then repeat the layers again, leeks, chicken and rice. Add half a teaspoon of salt and pour over enough milk to cover everything (about a pint). Cover closely and cook in a slow oven, Reg 2/150°, for 1–1½ hours depending on the chicken. This makes a lovely winter lunch.

For 4

CHICKEN CURRY

1 small roasting chicken
3 onions, peeled and chopped
1 clove garlic peeled and chopped
½ teaspoon ground turmeric
½ teaspoon ground chilli
½ teaspoon salt
2 teaspoons ground coriander
½ teaspoon cumin
¼ teaspoon each ground cinnamon, cloves and cardamom
pinch black pepper
4 tablespoons yoghurt olive oil

Heat the oil in a saucepan with a lid, and saute the onions and garlic for a few minutes. Add the chicken, cut in pieces and skinned, and the turmeric, chilli and salt, and saute until the chicken is lightly browned, five to seven minutes. Add the coriander, cinnamon, cloves, cardamom, cumin and yoghurt, and fry three minutes more. Simmer covered for one hour, adding a little water if necessary. Serve with plenty of rice and Raita and Dhal.

For 4–5

CHICKEN PAPRIKA

An elderly chicken, jointed
2–3 onions, chopped
2 tablespoons oil and butter, or chicken fat
2 tablespoons paprika
¼ pint sour cream

Brown the pieces of chicken in oil and butter or chicken fat, in a flameproof casserole, remove them to a dish and fry the onions in the same fat. Stir in the paprika, let it cook for a minute, then return the chicken, season and cover very tightly with foil and the pan lid. Leave to simmer very slowly or put in a low oven, Reg 2½/155°, for 1–1½ hours, depending on the age of the chicken. When it is tender, thicken the copious juice with half the sour cream just before serving (don't let it boil), Serve each helping with an extra dollop of sour cream and a sprinkling Of paprika on top. Boiled noodles tossed in butter are lovely with this dish.

For 4

GRILLED PIGEON

one young pigeon per person (available from March to October)
salt, pepper and lemon juice
butter
dried breadcrumbs
Dijon mustard

Choose small pigeons in the hope that these are young and therefore tender. Cut them through the backbone, split them open and flatten them like an open book. Season with salt and pepper and sprinkle with lemon juice.

Dot with butter, and grill under medium heat, on the skin side first; turn after 5–10 minutes, and spoon the other side with the melted butter. Dab it with mustard and sprinkle with breadcrumbs as soon as it is gently browned; turn once more to the outside, dot with mustard, baste with butter and sprinkle with more breadcrumbs ; cook gently until slightly crisp and golden. Serve with mustard sauce (page 139) and watercress.

BRAISED PIGEONS WITH CELERY SAUCE

4 young pigeons
flour
2 heads celery
2 onions
2 oz bacon in a piece
butter
1 glass red wine
thyme, bayleaf
3 or 4 tablespoons cream
1 tablespoon beurre manié (page 173)
a little salt and plenty of freshly ground pepper

Cut the celery into half-inch pieces and chop the onions coarsely. Cut the bacon into rough dice.

Heat the butter in a flameproof casserole, add the bacon, and when it is sizzling brown the pigeons, dusted in flour, in the fat for a few minutes, until they are coloured on every side. Remove them to a plate and put the vegetables into the casserole to sweat, covered, for a few minutes. Lay the pigeons on top and pour the heated wine over everything. Add herbs, salt and pepper, cover and simmer on top of the stove or in the oven at Reg 3/160°, so that the liquid is almost, but not quite, boiling, for about 1½ hours, or until the pigeons are tender. Put the birds on a hot dish and keep warm with the vegetables, scooped out of the sauce. Skim most of the fat off the juices and thicken them with the beurre manie, stirring all the time. The juice is copious, most of it coming from the celery. Finish the sauce by stirring in the cream, and taste for seasoning. Pour it over the birds and vegetables and serve pureed potatoes.

Alternatively, put a pint of fresh shelled peas and a lettuce into the pot, instead of the celery, about 25–30 minutes before the end of the cooking.

For 4

RABBIT STEW

1 small rabbit
6 oz fresh belly of pork
1 onion, finely chopped
butter and oil forfrying
1 glass white wine
1 ½ lbs tomatoes, peeled and chopped
1 bunch parsley, tied with thread
1 clove garlic, chopped
salt and freshly ground pepper
parsley and garlic to finish

Remove the rind and cut the pork into cubes; sizzle it in the oil and butter in a saute pan until the fat begins to run. Add the onion and soften it, browning only slightly. Add the jointed rabbit and brown the pieces thoroughly. Bring the wine to the boil in a small pan. Pour it over the rabbit and add the tomatoes, parsley, garlic, salt and pepper.

Turn the heat down and simmer uncovered, stirring from time to time and turning the pieces of rabbit, for 1–1½ hours until the rabbit is tender.

Serve in a gratin dish, spooning the pork and tomatoes over the rabbit and sprinkle with freshly chopped parsley and garlic.

For 4

SAUTÉ OF RABBIT WITH MUSTARD

1 tender young rabbit jointed, and its liver
butter and oil for frying
2 shallots, sliced into rings
2 rashers bacon, rinds removed, cut in pieces
1 glass white wine
generous sprig thyme
salt and freshly ground pepper
parsley, chopped
single cream
2 teaspoons Dijon mustard

Melt enough butter and oil in a large shallow frying pan or casserole to cover the base of the pan. Fry the shallots for a minute, add the bacon, then turn up the heat and brown the rabbit pieces, keeping the liver aside. Add the wine and let it bubble a little, turn down the heat, add the thyme, salt and pepper, and let the rabbit cook, covered, until it is tender, which should be within half an hour or even less if it is a really young one. Remove the sprig of thyme.

Fry the liver in butter, chop or slice it and mix it with the cream and mustard. Pour this over the rabbit pieces, heat through, reduce by boiling'if necessary, and serve sprinkled with parsley.

If you have a tough or large rabbit, cook it much longer. Flour the pieces before frying, and after the wine has bubbled up add half a pint of warm stock, which can be made from the head and giblets of the rabbit. Simmer until tender and then proceed as before to finish the sauce.

If the sauce is not thick enough, add an egg yolk or beurre manié (page 173), or reduce by boiling rapidly.

RABBIT ESCALOPES

2 fillets from either side of the backbone of a large, tender rabbit
seasoned flour
1 egg, beaten
fine dried breadcrumbs
1 tablespoon each of butter and oil
butter
dash of sherry

Ask the butcher to take the fillets from the rabbit before he joints it. If he refuses, take it home whole, and with a sharp, pointed knife cut a line as near the spine as you can, all along the back. Keep the knife against the bone and carefully remove the fillet. The underbelly, which is thin and flappy, will come too; cut this off. Turn the fillets underside up, so the silvery side is below, and cut lengthwise almost through but not quite. Lay them on a piece of well-oiled greaseproof paper, cover with another piece and then bash, with either a proper steak beater or a rolling pin. They will flatten out considerably to a neat pear shape.

Take them out of the paper, dip in seasoned flour, then beaten egg, then crumbs. Fry gently in butter and oil for about five minutes each side.

Remove them to a warm plate while you drop another tablespoon of butter into the pan, raise the heat, and as it froths add a dash of sherry. Stir it quickly and pour a little of this good gravy on each escalope.

This is only feasible if you have a large rabbit. Use the rest for a pate, stew, pie or jelly.

For 2

ROAST SADDLE OF HARE

1 saddle of hare, preferably marinated for two days as this makes it more tender and tasty and improves the flavour of the gravy
flour
4 rashers bacon
butter, beef dripping or pork fat
water
salt and freshly ground pepper
½ pint single cream

Take the hare out of the marinade and wipe it dry. Remove the silvery membrane over the back with a sharp knife. Preheat the oven to Reg 7/220°. Melt about half an ounce of butter in a frying pan. Dust the saddle with flour, brown it on all sides in the butter, take it out and wrap in bacon rashers. Roast in butter for 20–30 minutes, basting often. Add half a glass of water five minutes before it is cooked. Take off the bacon and put the hare with the rashers on a hot serving dish to keep warm.

Pour off some of the butter from the roasting tin, or scoop it off with a metal spoon. Add a minute sprinkling of flour to the juices in the tin; let it bubble a moment and stir in the cream. Heat gently, taste for seasoning, and pour the small amount of thickish sauce over the saddle.

Carve in lengthwise strips parallel to the backbone and serve with pureed potatoes or celeriac or hot beetroot.

Some people include the back legs to stretch the saddle further.

For 2–3

JUGGED HARE

1 hare, jointed and cut up
seasoned flour
2 tablespoons lard or dripping
1 large onion
4 carrots
1 stick celery
bunch of parsley and thyme
4 cloves
8 peppercorns
stock, salt
tablespoon beurre manie (page 173)
small glass port, or 1 tablespoon redcurrant jelly

If you like, you can marinate the hare for 24 hours in the marinade for game. Wipe the joints dry and flour thoroughly all over. Heat the lard in a flameproof casserole and fry the joints quickly to brown them.

Put them aside and put the sliced onion and the carrots and celery, cleaned and sliced, into the pan. Cover and allow to sweat for ten minutes. Replace the hare, add the herbs, cloves and peppercorns, and pour in enough stock just to cover. Add a little salt and simmer, covered, for one and a half hours, in the oven at Reg 2/150° or on top of the stove.

Remove the joints to a dish. Strain the liquid and reduce by almost half. Stir the beurre manie into the hare liquid making a smooth, thick sauce. Stir in the port or redcurrant jelly, put the hare back into the casserole or onto a nice white oval dish, and pour the sauce over.

Before serving allow it to stand in a hot place, without cooking, for ten minutes, to let the sauce and meat marry together again and the flavour develop.

If you have a large hare, keep the saddle to roast later; if a small one, include it.

For 4

MARINADE FOR GAME

¼ pint vinegar (wine or cider)
½ pint red wine
grating of nutmeg
bayleaf, sprig of thyme
2 large onions, finely sliced
salt and peppercorns

Mix everything together and pour it over the game in a china or glazed earthenware dish. Turn the meat over from time to time; you can leave it there from one to fourteen days.

VEGETABLES

The only way to buy fresh vegetables, unless you want to pay the earth for them, is in season, and to buy them often so that they can be eaten absolutely fresh. There are dozens of different vegetables to be seen trundling in muddy lorries towards Covent Garden on any dark winter morning; parsnips, cabbages, sprouts, beetroots, carrots, endives, celeriac, swedes, celery, Jerusalem artichokes, red cabbage, turnips, winter spinach, onions, leeks, cauliflowers, spring greens and curly kale are all grown in Britain and are far, far cheaper to serve than the smallest handful of imported French beans. So, of course, are all the pulses that are so comforting on a cold day. Lettuces seem to struggle up all the year round, but they do become more expensive in winter and taste of less.

The best vegetables are home-grown, and at least home-grown herbs are a possibility for everyone, since they can be planted out quite happily in the smallest window-box. Parsley is almost always on sale, so it makes sense to concentrate on the more unusual herbs, tarragon, basil, lovage, even thyme, rosemary, sage and chives which can be made to feel at home on a city windowsill.

Since tomatoes are only in season for a few months (home-grown ones from August to October), it is worth remembering that tinned Italian tomatoes always make a good substitute in cooking. They are grown in blazing sunshine and have a beautiful sweet flavour even after they have been in a tin.

Most books on nutrition suggest peeling vegetables thinly, as many of the vitamins lie close to the surface and thick peeling disposes of too many of them; for economy this is important too, though it is not a rare sight to see even quite experienced cooks carving off the peel of potatoes, carrots, turnips, parsnips and so on in great chunks.

Nutrition books also suggest conservative (loaded word) cooking of green vegetables such as broccoli, cabbage, peas, beans and brussels sprouts. Their method is to use from half to one inch of water so the vegetables are virtually cooked in steam. But if you just cover them with salted water and cook them for the minimum time, they come out tasting and looking so much better and fresher that people are bound to eat more to make up for vitamins that have escaped. Once they are cooked, drained and smothered in butter vegetables should be eaten straight away; they do not keep hot well, and lose their flavour and colour very fast.

With salads, there are two vital things that go wrong. One is that the salad is washed but not properly dried before the dressing goes on – the result, a soggy wasteland of tasteless wet green. Second, instead of being over-generous with oil and lubricating the salad to give it a wonderful unctuousness that contrasts with the crisp leaves, the vinegar (which should be wine or even cider but never malt) is overdone and the result gives the palate a violent shock. Put the dressing on a green salad at the last possible minute, it goes listless so fast. A handful of parsley, tarragon or chervil with stalks removed are a good addition to a green salad. Tomatoes aren't; make two separate salads instead of one jumbled one. Watercress makes a very good salad to accompany game or a juicy piece of beef, and is nearly always cheap.

ROAST JERUSALEM ARTICHOKES

1 ½ lbs Jerusalem artichokes
lard or pork fat

Cook them like roast potatoes, parboiling for 2–5 minutes before putting into the hot fat. Baste them, put them in the oven and cook on the shelf below the meat, or put them in the roasting tin round the meat. Cook for about 30–40 minutes, turning over carefully and basting once or twice.

Very good with roast pork. You can also cook parsnips like this.

For 6

AUBERGINE FRITTERS

4 large aubergines
fritter batter (page 56)
salt
deep oil for frying

Cut the aubergines in lengthwise slices, sprinkle with salt, and allow them to drain for half an hour or more. Wash and dry the slices and coat them with batter. Heat the oil in a deep frying pan and deepfry the aubergines to a golden brown. Drain very well before serving. These are excellent with lamb.

This recipe is also fine for courgettes.

For 6–8

BROAD BEANS IN THEIR OWN SAUCE

2–4 lbs broad beans, depending on their age
½ oz butter
½ oz flour
top of the milk
1 tablespoon finely chopped parsley, chervil or savory
lemon juice
salt

Pod the beans. If they are young and tender include a section of the pod around some of them. If they are old and tough make sure you remove the crescent attached to the bean, and even their outer skin.

Bring salted water to the boil and throw them in. When tender, strain, keep the beans warm and reserve the liquid. In another pan melt the butter, make a white roux with the flour and gradually stir in a cup of the liquid, the top of the milk and the chopped herbs of your choice. When you have a smooth sauce add the beans and a squeeze of lemon, season with salt if necessary, and serve.

For 4

BROAD BEANS IN OIL

1½ lbs broad beans, small and fresh
6 spring onions
3 tablespoons olive oil
½ lemon
salt and black pepper

Cut up the broad beans with their pods still on. Any that look tough or ropey should be shelled. Roughly chop the firm parts of the onions. Heat the oil in a thick saucepan, put in the beans and spring onions and sweat them very gently with the lid on for 10 or 15 minutes. Add the juice of half a lemon and half a cup of water, salt and pepper, and cook uncovered until soft, about an hour. If necessary add a little more water. They should be very tender with an intense flavour. Good hot or cold.

For 4

CHANG'S CABBAGE

1 ½ lbs cabbage, green or white
2 tablespoons oil
few drops soy sauce
1 teaspoon salt
3 teaspoons sugar
2 tablespoons vinegar

Mix the salt, sugar and vinegar together. Slice the cabbage as finely as you can, discarding the tough stalks and outer leaves. Wash well and then shake as dry as possible in a cloth, as you would salad. Heat the oil in a large frying pan over a fairly high heat, and when it is really hot (but not burning), fling in the cabbage. Keep it moving about with a wooden spoon. As soon as it is all covered with oil, shake a few drops of soy sauce over it, then pour on the vinegar mixture. Let it cook a minute or two and serve at once.

Children don't always like this, but adults like it as a change from universal plain boiled cabbage (though when boiled correctly it can be a really beautiful and delicious vegetable).

This is a sweet-sour cabbage, very Chinese but rather good with Shepherd's Pie or chops. It is also very quick – cooked in seconds.

For 6

GERMAN RED CABBAGE

1 medium-sized red cabbage
1–2 oz butter, 2 cloves garlic
1 large cooking apple, peeledand cut up
2 medium onions, peeled and sliced
bunch of thyme, parsley, and a bayleaf
grated orange rind or juice
1 teaspoon caraway seeds
pinch cinnamon, pinch nutmeg
salt and pepper
2 tablespoons brown sugar
small glass red wine (left-over is best as it becomes slightly vinegary)

Preheat oven to Reg 2/150°.

Take the large damaged outer leaves off the cabbage, quarter it and shred as finely as possible, discarding the centre core. Melt the butter in a flameproof casserole, add the cabbage and cook gently, covered; for five minutes. Add the apples, onions, garlic, a little grated orange rind, herbs, spices, salt and pepper. Mix everything together well, sprinkle on the sugar, add the wine, cover and put in the oven, for up to three hours. Check half-way through that it is not drying up, and if it is add a little hot water. This reheats very successfully, and is possibly even better for it.

A rich and filling dish.

For 4–6

RED CABBAGE FLAMANDE

1 medium red cabbage
2 eating apples, peeled and quartered
1 tablespoon caster sugar
2–3 tablespoons wine vinegar
salt, freshly ground pepper, and nutmeg
butter

Remove the outside leaves of the cabbage, cut it into quarters, cut out the stalk and slice the leaves into thin shreds. It shouldn't need washing. Put the sliced cabbage into a buttered casserole, with the apples, sprinkling the layers with the sugar, vinegar, salt, pepper and nutmeg. Cook, covered, at Reg 3/160° for 3–3½ hours. This mild, sweet dish of red cabbage is the perfect thing to serve with hare or any othfer game or with smoked boiling sausage, or frankfurters.

For 6

ITALIAN CARROTS

1 lb carrots, old or young
1 oz butter
4 teaspoon salt
4 teaspoon sugar
1 dessertspoon flour
4 pint water

Cut the cleaned carrots into thin strips. Melt the butter in a thick saucepan with a close-fitting lid. Sweat the carrots gently in the butter for about five minutes. Add salt and sugar and sprinkle on the flour, mixing it well with a wooden spoon. Then gradually add the water, clamp down the lid tightly, and leave to simmer slowly for twenty minutes. The carrots will be very tasty and covered with a thick golden sauce.

This recipe is also perfect for tiny young turnips and for celery. If you cook celery in this way, blanch it first in boiling salted water for five minutes

For 4

CARROTTES RAPÉES

1 large garden carrot for each person
6 tablespoons olive oil
1½ tablespoons white wine or cider vinegar
pinch of sugar, salt, and freshly ground pepper

Grate the carrots finely; make a dressing with the oil, vinegar, sugar, salt and pepper and turn the grated carrot in it until every shred is glistening. In France they might serve this half and half with celeriac rémoulade or a salad of very finely shredded red cabbage tossed in a dressing heavily loaded with Dijon mustard.

For 5–6

CELERIAC RÉMOULADE

2 heads celeriac
mayonnaise:
2 egg yolks
½ pint oil
vinegar (white wine or cider)
salt and freshly ground pepper
mustard powder

Make a very mustardy mayonnaise by combining a spoonful of mayonnaise with at least a teaspoonful of mustard powder, and mixing it very well into the rest.

Peel the celeriac and cut it into thin strips or shred it on a mandoline. Mix in the mayonnaise quickly.

It is quite common to blanch the shredded celeriac before adding the mayonnaise but this can make it soggy and spoil the flavour.

For 8

COURGETTES IN BUTTER

1½ lbs courgettes
2 oz butter
chopped parsley (or chervil, mint or chives)
salt and freshly ground pepper
lemon juice

Wash the courgettes and peel them if necessary.

Cut in half-inch rounds or quarter them lengthways, then cut these slices in half.

Bring a pan of salted water to the boil and cook the courgettes for five minutes. Drain well and return to the rinsed and dried pan with the butter.

Sprinkle with whichever herb you choose and simmer gently, without browning, until the courgettes are tender, 10-15 minutes. Season, and add a squeeze of lemon if you like.

For 4

COURGETTES AU GRATIN

6 small courgettes
4 medium tomatoes, peeled and chopped
1 clove garlic
parsley, chopped
salt and freshly ground pepper
1 oz butter
2 tablespoons oil
½ cup dried breadcrumbs

Don't peel the courgettes unless they are elderly. Slice into thick pennies and strew with salt, leaving them in a colander or on a tilted plate for an hour or so, to drain off some of their moisture.

Heat the oil and butter in a large frying pan, and toss the dried courgettes, a few at a time, without browning them. Keep them warm. Melt a little more butter and oil and cook the chopped tomatoes, garlic, salt, pepper and parsley, until you have a thickened puree. Add the courgettes and turn the mixture into a gratin dish. Cover with the breadcrumbs, dot with butter and cook in a hot oven, Reg 7/220°, for half an hour.

For 4 (or 2 if served as a course on its own)

CHICK PEAS

You cannot skimp the soaking of chick peas – they must be soaked overnight. Wash them first, then put them in a bowl large enough for them almost to double in size. Cover well with Water and after their soaking cook them gently in the same water. A pinch of bicarbonate of soda softens the water and shortens the cooking time (rain water is, in fact, the best thing to cook all pulses in). Add no salt until the peas are almost tender.

Cooking time depends on the age of the peas: new, they can take as little as half an hour, old, up to two hours.

HUMMUS WITH TAHINA

½ lb chick peas, soaked overnight
¼ pint tahina paste (made of sesame seeds and bought in tins or bottles from Greek or Cypriot shops)
juicy lemons
2 cloves garlic, crushed
salt
olive oil

The chick peas must be cooked very well (this page); drain them and reserve their liquid. Greeks then roll them with a rolling pin (in a large plastic bag) until they are pulverised, which gives an uneven texture but your can mouli or liquidise them, moistened with a little of their liquid. When they are crushed, add more of the cooking liquid, the tahina paste, lemon juice, crushed garlic and salt. The taste must be adjusted to the way you like it, some like more lemon, some more garlic and so on. Serve, moistened with a little more oil, on a plate, with a few spring onions and some good hot bread. Eat this as a simple lunch dish or a first course.

For 6

CRUDITÉS WITH AIOLI

6–8 carrots
2 green peppers
2 heads chicory
1 cucumber
6 sticks celery
6 tomatoes
2 heads fennel
aioli (page 136)

This can be made with any fresh crisp vegetables. Simply clean and cut them up, the carrots, peppers, chicory, cucumber and celery into sticks about two inches long, the tomatoes into quarters, the fennel into slices.

Put the vegetables, each sort in a group, on a large dish that just holds them all. Cover and chill lightly; serve crisp and fresh with a powerful aioli, as the first course to an otherwise rich meal. Eat them with your fingers, dipping each piece into a dollop of aioli on your plate.

For 6

DANDELION SALAD

A handful of tender young dandelion leaves
chives, spring onions or mild onion, chopped
1 clove of garlic
2 tablespoons oil
1 teaspoon sugar
pinch of salt

Wash the leaves well and cut the stalks short. Shake them dry, put them in a salad bowl and sprinkle with chives, spring onion or mild onion. Pulverise the garlic, add oil, sugar and salt and toss into the salad. The dandelions are bitter, but if you want a sharper taste, add a little lemon juice to the dressing.

Ancient herb-lore says that if you select a healthy young dandelion plant in the garden and lay a slate or brick over it, the leaves will continue growing and blanch themselves, which will make them more tender and less bitter.

For 2

BULGOUR

½ lb coarsely ground wheat
¼ lb Italian vermicelli
1 pint hot stock, bouillon or water
2–3 oz butter
salt
pepper
sprinkle of parsley

A deep, round earthenware dish with a lid is good for cooking this in. Otherwise, use a largish pan with a lid. Melt the butter in the pan. Break up the vermicelli, and brown it in the butter, stirring with a wooden spoon. Add the ground wheat (bulgour) and stir while it rapidly absorbs the butter. Pour in the hot stock or water, stir well and, putting the lid on, turn the heat as low as you can. Let it cook undisturbed for 12 minutes, when all the liquid should be absorbed. Stir again, and replace lid. Remove from heat and leave it alone for another 12 minutes. Stir it again and leave it for 5 minutes.

Serve with seasoning of more pepper than salt, sprinkled with parsley, and if liked, a spoonful of yoghurt with each helping.

Similar to couscous, it goes well with stews.

For 6–8

TO COOK DRIED BEANS OR LENTILS

white, green, red, brown or black, large or small beans, 3 oz per person
water
bouquet of parsley, thyme, bayleaf, celery stalk and garlic if liked
salt

Soak the beans for several hours, at least four and at most twelve or overnight; any longer and they will start to ferment. Drain and put in a saucepan with enough cold water to come two inches above the top of the beans. Add no salt but put in the herbs and garlic. Bring slowly to the boil and cook gently until the beans are tender, a minimum of one hour and up to two. If they take longer than this the chances are they will never be tender. Add salt about 15 minutes before draining the beans.

They can be served as they are with plenty of freshly chopped parsley and butter; or bathed in a sauce of tomatoes and onion cooked in oil with a cupful of their own liquid; or stirred into a creamy sauce made with butter, flour and their own liquid, plus chopped parsley; or you can leave out the parsley but add chopped boiled bacon or ham. Cold, they make very good salads with vinaigrette dressing and raw onion, tuna fish, green beans or just parsley.

HARICOT AND FRENCH BEAN SALAD

½ lb large white haricot beans (dried)
1 onion
2 cloves garlic
1 lb French beans
1 tablespoon white wine vinegar
5–6 tablespoons olive oil
½ Spanish onion
parsley, chopped
salt and freshly ground pepper

Soak the beans for about 5-6 hours. Put them in a pan and cover well with cold water, put in the peeled onion and the cloves of garlic. Bring slowly to the boil, skim and simmer for about f hour. Add salt and simmer on for a quarter of an hour or so. When tender but not mushy, drain and cool. Cook the French beans, broken in pieces if they are too long, in boiling salted water for 10–15 minutes. When just tender, strain and refresh quickly under the cold tap. Drain very well. Mix the two kinds of beans together. Make an oily dressing with plenty of freshly ground pepper, and mix it in carefully so as not to break up the haricots. Strew some rings of Spanish onion on top and some chopped parsley if you like.

This is a very pretty dish.

For 6

DHAL

½ lb small orange lentils
1 onion, peeled and chopped
1 clove of garlic, peeled and chopped
1 oz butter, or margarine and oil
1 teaspoon tomato puree
½ teaspoon coriander powder
½ teaspoon cumin seed
salt

Cover the lentils (they don't need soaking) with double their volume of water. They will cook quite quickly and absorb most of it. In another pan, fry the onion and garlic lightly in the butter until transparent. Add the tomato puree, spices and some salt. Stir. Add the lentils, which should not be too runny. Mix all well together and cook until the flavours are absorbed by the lentils (5–10 minutes). This will reheat well. If it is too stiff, add hot water.

For eating with curries.

For 4

LEEKS IN RED WINE

10 leeks, the same size and not too large
2 tablespoons olive oil
1 glass red wine
½ pint boiling water or stock
salt

Trim the leeks and wash well. Drain and shake them as dry as possible. Heat the oil in a wide shallow pan with room for all the leeks side by side. Gently brown them all over, pour on the wine and let it bubble a minute or two. Add salt and boiling stock or water, cover the pan and cook until the leeks are tender (test by piercing the root end with a sharp knife).

Take out the leeks with a perforated spoon and put them on a hot serving dish. Reduce the liquid a little and pour it over. These are particularly good with roast meat or chicken.

For 4

LEEKS VINAIGRETTE

1½ lbs of the smallest leeks you can buy
5 dessertspoons olive oil
1½ dessertspoons white wine vinegar
salt and freshly ground pepper
Dijon mustard
garlic

Clean and trim the leeks, keeping the firm white part and the best of the green.

Bring a pan of salted water to the boil, drop in the leeks and let them cook until just tender. Put in a colander and leave to drain and cool.

Mash a clove of garlic with salt, mix with a teaspoon of mustard and plenty of pepper. Add 1½ dessertspoons of vinegar and mix in thoroughly. Now add the oil, mixing gradually – it thickens like mayonnaise. You will need about 5 dessertspoons of oil but taste from time to time until it is right. When the leeks are thoroughly drained, lay them on a plate all in the same direction. Pour on the dressing and turn them a couple of times. They look very good on a white oval or oblong dish.

Serve these as an hors d'oeuvre or salad.

For 2–4

MUSHROOMS A LA GRECQUE

¾ lb button mushrooms
4 tablespoons olive oil
4 tablespoons water
juice of ½ lemon
1 teaspoon coriander seeds
salt and freshly groundpepper
bayleaf, thyme, parsley

Boil together in a wide shallow pan the oil, water, lemon juice, coriander seeds, seasoning and a large bunch of herbs, for ten minutes.

Clean the mushrooms, and if they are small add them whole to the liquid, if large, quarter them first. They must be closed and round; open ones absorb too much liquid, and exude too much so they end up sloppy. Simmer the mushrooms slowly for ten minutes, stirring, then remove them to a dish and reduce the liquid a little. Pour it over the mushrooms, when the herbs and coriander seeds will be stranded on top.

Leave them there, they look lovely and improve the flavour. Let the mushrooms get cold and eat with coarse brown bread and unsalted butter. They do shrink terribly but they don't need to be eaten in large quantities. Serve them with other salads as an hors d'oeuvre. They are good with cold cooked lentils in an oil and vinegar dressing, or with courgettes done in the same way as the mushrooms but with tomatoes instead of water added to the sauce.

For 4

RAW MUSHROOM SALAD

½ lb tiny button mushrooms
¼ pint sour cream
½ lemon
salt and freshly ground pepper

Trim the mushrooms, and if they are the slightest bit bruised or brown, peel them. As you peel each one, rub it with a cut lemon. When they are all ready slice each one down into very thin slices. Keep the stalks on so that each slice shows a tiny mushroom in section.

Put them into a white china or earthenware bowl and mix in the sour cream; season lightly. This should be a very delicate salad. If you like you can add a little more lemon juice to sharpen it up.

This is one of the prettiest salads there is.

For 3

FIELD MUSHROOMS

mushrooms
butter
top of the milk
salt
pepper

Clean and slice the mushrooms, melt the butter in a frying pan and fry them gently. As they absorb the butter, add a saucerful of creamy milk.

Continue cooking for about ten minutes; they will then take more milk. This, rather than being absorbed, will thicken a little, leaving the mushrooms in a delicate creamy sauce. Add salt and pepperto taste and eat at once with egg and bacon or toast.

The quantities depend on how many mushrooms you find.

MUSHROOMS WITH BROWN RICE

½ lb mushrooms
4 oz brown rice
1 oz butter
parsley
3 cloves garlic
salt and freshly ground pepper

Soak the brown rice in salted water overnight, strain and rinse. Put it in fresh salted water and cook gently until tender, 15–20 minutes. The grains should still be separate and have a slight bite to them.

Meanwhile slice the mushrooms and put them in a saute pan with the butter. Let them cook very, very slowly so that the juices all run out; stir from time to time. Chop the parsley and garlic finely.

Stir the drained rice and the parsley and garlic into the mushrooms, season, let it get really hot and then serve with stewed lamb or beef or roast lamb.

For 4

REALLY CRISP FRIED ONIONS

Spanish onions
salt
flour
deep fat or oil

Slice the onions into thin rings and separate each one. Sprinkle lightly with fine salt and let them stand for an hour or so, for the moisture to drain off. Toss them in flour and drop them into hot fat or oil (with blue haze rising). As soon as they are golden brown take them out and drain them on kitchen paper. Eat as they are or with hamburgers etc.

POMMES DE TERRE RISSOLÉES

2 lbs new potatoes the size of a walnut
2-3 oz butter, preferably clarified (page 173) or unsalted
coarse salt

Scrape the potatoes, and dry each one thoroughly on a cloth. Melt the butter in a large heavy saucepan and fry the potatoes, turning them over and over so they brown evenly. When they are nicely golden turn the heat right down and cover the saucepan. Let them cook gently like this for an hour. When the potatoes are tender, and easily pierced with a skewer, turn up the heat and shake the pan until they are crisp on the outside. It may take several minutes, so take care not to burn the butter at this point. As soon as they are crisp, sprinkle with plenty of coarse salt, and serve. They don't always end up absolutely crisp, but they do always end up absolutely delicious.

This is a recipe for small new potatoes; very good with any plainly roasted or braised poultry or meat.

For 6

POTATO CRISPS

1 large potato
salt
deep oil for frying

Peel and slice the potato as thinly as possible. This is quickly done on a cucumber slicer or mandoline. Wash the potato slices under the cold tap as you cut them, to remove the loose starch granules, and keep them all in cold water until you have finished the slicing. Then dry well in a cloth, shaking them as if you were drying a salad. Keep them in the cloth until ready to start frying.

Heat the oil in a pan with a deep-frying basket; when a blue haze rises test one slice. If it comes straight up to the surface, sizzling, the oil is ready. Lift the basket out of the oil, holding it over the pan fill it with two handfuls of crisps, and lower it back into the oil. If you put in too many crisps there is a great danger of the oil boiling over, so be very careful at this point and whisk the basket out if the oil starts to rise too far. As soon as the crisps start to colour lift the basket out of the oil while you count ten, then put it back again. As they turn golden lift them out, let them drain, and put them in a dish lined with kitchen paper to dry, sprinkling with fine salt.

They keep crisp in polythene bags.

PERFECT MASHED POTATOES

1½ lbs good floury potatoes
½ pint milk
2 oz butter
salt freshly ground pepper, and a grating of nutmeg

Cook the potatoes in boiling salted water. It doesn't matter whether you peel the potatoes before or after they are cooked, but they should be more or less the same size and cooked very thoroughly indeed. Once they are peeled, cooked and drained, put them back in the saucepan over a very low heat to dry out for a minute. Mash with a fork or potato masher,, or for real perfection put them through the mouli, before adding hot milk and butter, beating with a fork or wooden spoon as you go. Season with salt, pepper and nutmeg. The result should be really light. If it seems too dry add more milk and butter.

For 4

GERMAN POTATO DROPSCONES

¼ lb potatoes, peeled
¼ lb plain flour and 1 heaped teaspoon baking powder, or ¼ lb self-raising flour
2 eggs, separated
1 tablespoon oil or melted butter
¼ pint or less of milk
salt

Grate the raw potatoes. Squeeze out some of their liquid and put them into a bowl. Mix at once with the flour and baking powder. Incorporate the egg yolks, butter or oil, milk and a little salt. Whip the egg whites stiffly, and fold into the mixture.

Heat and grease the griddle and drop spoonfuls of the mixture on to the griddle, giving them about three minutes on each side. Serve with eggs and bacon. They are also good spread with butter.

About 20 scones

POTATO CAKES

mashed potato
1 beaten egg
self-raising flour, not more than half as much as potato
salt and freshly ground pepper
bacon fat or beef dripping

Mix the potatoes, egg, flour and seasoning to make a firm dough. Roll out to about half an inch thick and cut into rounds. Fry well, in hot fat quarter of an inch deep in the frying pan. Delicious for breakfast, with egg and bacon, or for children's high tea. Surprisingly, creamy mashed potato is less successful than dry mashed potato.

The number depends on the amount of left-over mashed potato you have.

CHAMP

2 lbs potatoes
¼–½ pint milk
butter
salt and pepper
10 spring onions
bunch parsley

Peel and cut up the potatoes, and cook them with plenty of salt for a bit too long, until they are really soft but not disintegrating. It takes about 25 minutes. Meanwhile chop the spring onions and parsley as finely as you can, and heat the milk. When the potatoes are done, drain them and mash them with the boiling milk, pepper and more salt if necessary, plus butter if you like. When they are finely pureed add the chopped onions and parsley and mash these in. The potatoes should still be moist enough to fall off the spoon when you give it a shake.

This is an Irish potato dish which you could practically eat on its own. It is also very good with fish or any plain roasted meat.

For 6

PERSIAN RICE

3 oz rice per person
2 oz butter
1 tablespoon salt

Pour a kettle of boiling water over the rice in a sieve. Separate the grains and soak for three or four hours in cold water. Wash thoroughly and put in a large pan with copious amounts of cold water and a tablespoon of salt. Boil for exactly eight minutes, until the rice is almost, but not quite, tender. Wash again under the cold tap and drain.

Put one ounce of melted butter in a flameproof casserole and put in the drained rice. Pour over another ounce of melted butter, cover with a cloth and then with the casserole lid. Put over a very low flame for 15–20 minutes. Each grain is separate, perfectly cooked and delicious. At the bottom of the pan is a golden crust which is much sought after by the Persians.

This is a complicated way of rice-cooking, but very good. You can leave out some of the soaking, if you don't have time.

Use Basmati or best Patna rice. These are the best quality, long-grain rices and more likely to cook to perfection than nameless packets or semi-prepared brands.

For 4–6

RISOTTO MILANESE

12 oz Italian rice
2–3 tablespoons olive oil
1 small onion, chopped
small glass white wine
pinch saffron
¾–1 pint bouillon or light stock, heated
salt and freshly ground pepper
knob of butter
2–3 oz Parmesan, freshly grated

Heat the oil in a fairly large saute pan with a lid, and fry the onion gently until it is transparent. Add the rice and stir with a wooden spoon, until it too is transparent. Stir the saffron into the wine and add it to the rice; let it sizzle, then add ¾ pint of hot stock, turn the heat low, cover and leave it to cook about 15 minutes. Check that it is not sticking to the bottom; if it is, it needs another cup of stock or water.

After 20–30 minutes the rice should be quite soft, and all the liquid absorbed. Stir in the lump of butter and a spoonful or two of grated Parmesan. Serve with more butter and Parmesan on each helping, and some black pepper. It is very good on its own, but you can serve it with kebabs (page 97) or chicken livers.

For 4

RAITA

½ large cucumber or 1 small whole one
1 dove garlic
small sprig mint
½ teaspoon salt
1 5-oz pot plain yoghurt

Peel the cucumber, then, according to how you like it, grate it or cut it in small cubes or sticks; thin round slices don't suit this dish at all.

Crush the garlic in a garlic crusher or chop as finely as you can. Slice the mint leaves finely. Sprinkle the cucumber with the mint, garlic and salt and leave it to drain in a strainer for half an hour.

Put it in a bowl, mix with the yoghurt and chill until needed. In India it is usually grated; in Greece cut in little chunks. You can skip the half hour's draining if in a hurry, but don't wait too long before eating it or the yoghurt will become watery. The draining also makes it more digestible.

A soothing dish to accompany curry and also a cool summer salad.

For 2

SALADE AU LARD

Chicory, young spinach leaves, dandelion, endive, or watercress
Vinaigrette dressing (page 143)
1 rasher of bacon per person

Wash the salad leaves and dry well. Trim the rind off the bacon and cut into little sticks about half an inch long. Fry the rinds slowly in a frying pan to extract the fat; when it starts to run remove the rinds and fry the bacon pieces until crisp and brown, while you are making a slightly vinegary dressing; don't add much salt, the bacon will do this.

Toss the salad in the dressing and at the last moment pour the bacon and its fat over everything. Mix well and serve with the bacon still hot.

For any number

SPINACH AND CHICK PEAS

½ lb chick peas
salt
1 lb spinach
1 tablespoon paprika
2 tablespoons olive oil
1 slice bread
1 onion, chopped
3–4 tomatoes, peeled and chopped
1 clove garlic

Soak the chick peas overnight and cook as on page 119. When they are tender, fry the slice of bread golden in oil. Put the fried bread on one side while you fry the onions, then the tomatoes. Wash the spinach, shake it and sprinkle it with salt.

Heat two tablespoons of oil in a large pan, add the paprika and stir it in. Add the spinach and when it is lightly fried, put the mixture into a saucepan with the chick peas, onions and tomatoes.

Pound the clove of garlic, add the fried bread and pound it thoroughly. Add this mixture to the chick peas. Cover and simmer for half an hour, when you will have a fragrant vegetable stew, thickened and interestingly flavoured by the pounded fried bread.

Very good for a cold day.

For 3—4

SPINACH WITH TOMATO SAUCE

1 lb spinach
½ lb tomatoes
salt and freshly ground pepper
pinch sugar
1 small onion, chopped
1–2 oz butter
butter and oil forfrying

Wash the spinach very well, shake off most of the water and cook in a covered pan with the moisture still clinging to the leaves, until tender, 10–15 minutes. Drain off the water it has made, chop and stir in the butter and a little salt.

While the spinach is cooking, skin and chop the tomatoes. Sweat the chopped onion in a little butter and oil, without browning, for 10–15 minutes. Add the tomatoes, salt, pepper and sugar to taste. Let it simmer into a rough puree, stirring from time to time.

Serve the spinach with a little dollop of tomato sauce in the centre of each helping, so it looks like a red and green fried egg.

It is a surprisingly good combination of tastes.

For 2

SPINACH TART

2 lbs fresh spinach
1 oz butter
1 oz flour
½ pint creamy milk
2 cloves garlic
1 oz grated Parmesan
butter
salt and freshly ground pepper
9 oz flan pastry (page 172)

Make the pastry well in advance and keep it in a cool place. Cook the washed spinach in the water still clinging to the leaves, with a good sprinkling of salt. Make a smooth Bechamel sauce with the butter flour and milk; season it and add the crushed cloves of garlic and most of the cheese. Drain the spinach when it is well cooked, squeezing out the water very thoroughly, and chop slightly. Meanwhile butter a 7–8 inch flan case and line it with pastry. Bake this shell blind.

Mix the spinach into the sauce, pour into the flan case and sprinkle with the remaining cheese. Bake at Reg 4/180° for 15–20 minutes and brown the top briefly under the grill, dotting it with butter first.

This is a very good hot lunch dish; eaten cold it is marvellous for a picnic.

For 4

MASHED SWEDE

1 large swede
salt and pepper
sugar
1 oz butter
orange juice

Peel the swede, removing all the fibrous pieces. Cut into one-inch cubes, cover with cold water, add salt and cook 20–25 minutes. Drain the swede, mash carefully, add pepper, a little more salt if necessary, a sprinkling of sugar, the butter and, if you like, a squeeze of orange juice. Heat through and serve. Children seem to like this as much as carrots.

For 4–6

BAKED SWEDE

1 swede, peeled and cubed
2 oz butter
½ teaspoon salt
½ teaspoon sugar

Butter a small casserole with a close-fitting lid. Sprinkle the salt on to the cubed swede, and put it into the casserole, dotted with the remaining butter.

Sprinkle with the sugar, cover very tightly with foil and the lid, for you add no water, and bake in a low oven, or the bottom of a warm oven, for 1½ hours.

People with an aversion to mashed swede seem to gobble this up.

For 4

TO PEEL AND DE-SEED TOMATOES

Put the kettle on. Put the tomatoes (without their stalks) in a deep bowl. When the kettle boils, pour the water over them. Scoop them but one at a time with a spoon and peel them as quickly as you can. If there are a great many to skin, do them in several batches, as standing in hot water makes them mushy.

If you only have one or two tomatoes to peel, and a gas cooker, stick them on a fork and hold them over a burner. Turn the flame up high and turn the tomato in it until the skin pops, singes and splits; it will then peel off quite easily.

To remove the seeds: cut the tomato in half and hold one half in the palm of your hand. Squeezing it slightly, give it a brisk shake and the seeds will flop out.

To draw out the excess moisture: if you want to make stuffed tomatoes you can get rid of some of the water by sprinkling the insides of the halves with salt and leaving them upside-down to drain for half an hour or so.

STUFFED TOMATOES

6 large or 12 small tomatoes
2 oz butter
2 oz fresh breadcrumbs
12 leaves of basil or 1 teaspoon dried basil
6 black olives, stoned and chopped
2–3 cloves garlic
salt and freshly ground pepper

Melt the butter and mix it into the breadcrumbs. Add the finely chopped olives and basil, crushed cloves of garlic, salt and pepper. Mix together well. Cut the tomatoes in half across their equators. Empty out the seeds (see opposite) and put generous teaspoon of stuffing in each, pressing it with the back of the spoon. Bake at Reg 3/160° for one hour in an earthenware dish or baking tin. Serve them hot or cold.

These are to eat with lamb etc. or even on their own.

For 6

TOMATO AND MOZZARELLA SALAD

4 tomatoes
1 Mozzarella cheese
basil or oregano
salt and freshly ground pepper
oil and vinegar

Slice the cheese into rounds and lay a slice of tomato on top of each, or lay in overlapping lines, alternating tomato and Mozzarella, on a dish. Sprinkle with fresh or dried basil or oregano. Serve straight away with oil, vinegar, salt and pepper.

For 2

PLAIN TOMATO SALAD

1 lb firm, under- rather than over-ripe tomatoes
1 small onion
salt and pepper
2–3 tablespoons olive oil
sprinkling of fresh chopped parsley, basil or chives

For a delicate salad dip the tomatoes in boiling water as briefly as possible and skin them quickly. Slice them thinly across and lay the slices on a plate. Sprinkle lightly with salt. Treat the onions, also thinly sliced, in the same way.

When they have stood in the salt for ½–1 hour, tip the plates and drain off the juices. Rinse the onions, dry them, and scatter them over the tomatoes. Sprinkle with parsley and chives or basil. Add the oil and a turn of pepper, and serve chilled. Don't let it stand too long or the tomatoes lose their firm texture.

For 4

STUFFINGS AND SAUCES

It is a bore making a stuffing when you are roasting a bird, but it is worth it when you find it later, a bonus as it were. Not only turkeys deserve this treatment; some fish and lots of vegetables take well to a stuffing, and so of course do chickens and boned shoulders and breasts of lamb and veal.

Even a cut onion or lemon and a bunch of herbs help to keep a bird moist, but if you are going in for the real bona fide filling-stuffing you can choose from these categories, using a combination that suits the dish:

1. To keep it moist: bacon, mushrooms, onions, celery, apples, prunes.

2. To pad it out : breadcrumbs, rice, oats, cracked wheat, sausage meat.

3. To bind it: stock, tomato purée, butter, olive oil, egg, wine, milk, suet.

4. To flavour it: garlic, herbs, seasoning, spices, lemon peel or juice, pine nuts, chestnuts, almonds, raisins.

If you are stuffing vegetables, use part of the flesh that you remove to make room for the stuffing, and add minced beef, pork or lamb, chicken livers or diced bacon or ham.

Sauces were originally invented to disguise what the food was really like, and are now supposed to complement it. Certainly lots of dishes would be sadly lacking love if no sauce was made to go with them. The basic sauces are the very first things to be learned in domestic science lessons, and once you have bechamel, mayonnaise, hollandaise and basic tomato sauce under your beit, you can tackle almost anything. Sauces which use egg yolks to thicken them are the most difficult to handle because of the curdling, but with practice they go quite fast, and although fiddly and a bit extravagant, they add a great touch of luxury to simple food.

BECHAMEL SAUCE

1 oz butter
1 oz flour
½ pint milk
salt pepper

Heat the milk to just below boiling point (see note below on infusion). Melt the butter in a small saucepan over a moderate heat without browning.

Tip in the flour and stir to amalgamate it with the butter. This mixture is called a white roux and should not be allowed to brown. When it starts to honeycomb – i.e. when small bubbles start to break all over the surface of the mixture – pour in one third of the milk, stirring vigorously until you have a smooth mixture. When it has thickened into a smooth paste add one third more milk. Stir again and when it has thickened gradually add the rest of the milk until you have a smooth sauce of the consistency you require. Season and cook very gently, stirring from time to time, for five minutes, to cook the flour. The best Bechamel is made with milk which you have previously infused with various flavourings to make it tastier. Simply put a small sliced onion, a bayleaf, a small bunch of parsley and a few peppercorns into the cold milk, bring it to boiling point, turn the heat right down and let the milk stand just not boiling over a very low flame for up to half an hour. Strain the milk before you make the sauce.

This makes ½ pint, medium thick sauce.

EGG SAUCE

½ pint well-flavoured thin Bechamel, made with half milk and half fish- or chicken-stock
2 hard-boiled eggs
salt and white pepper

Sieve the egg yolks into the Bechamel, chop the whites and add these too. The Bechamel should be of a creamy consistency so that the egg whites are visible as a texture in the sauce. Season and serve hot. This has become almost a joke because it smacks of institutions, but made properly it is a good English sauce of quality.

A delicate sauce for chicken, fishcakes and steamed cod, turbot or halibut.

SAUCE HOLLANDAISE

2 tablespoons white wine vinegar
1 tablespoon water
2–3 peppercorns
4 bayleaf
1 blade mace
1 large egg yolk
4–5 oz slightly salted butter

Cut the butter into small cubes and if it is very hard let it soften a bit. Put the vinegar, water, peppercorns, bayleaf and mace into a small saucepan and reduce to half their quantity. Allow to cool and remove peppercorns, bayleaf and mace. Take a double saucepan, or a pan into which a suitable bowl or basin will fit, and heat some water in it to just below boiling point. In order to lessen the risk of the sauce curdling keep the water below the boil, and make sure it doesn't actually touch the base of the bowl or pan in which the sauce is cooking. Using the bowl or pan which is to go over the water, mix the reduced vinegar and water with the egg yolk and a cube of the soft butter. Place it over the hot water and stirring all the time with a wooden spoon, add the cubes of butter one at a time, letting each one melt before you add another.

If the sauce shows signs of thickening too fast, or curdling, remove it at once from the water. If it is too thick add a few drops of water or the top of the milk. Taste for salt. If it is too sharp add some unsalted butter. It should be smooth and fairly thick, and is served lukewarm.

For serving with Oeufs Bénédictine and poached fish (and asparagus).

HORSERADISH SAUCE

1–2 tablespoons grated horseradish
4 teaspoon salt
4 teaspoon mustard powder
1 teaspoon white sugar
1 dessertspoon wine vinegar or lemon juice
2–3 tablespoons thin cream or top of the milk

Mix all well together. The grating of fresh horseradish is far more of a torture than cutting up onions, but the result is really worth it. Beware if you start growing it in the garden; it must be confined, otherwise the whole garden will soon be covered with what is virtually an indestructible weed.

For hot or cold roast beef, or herrings.

MAYONNAISE

1 egg yolk
¼ pint olive oil
salt and white pepper
1 teaspoon lemon juice or white wine vinegar

Put the egg yolk with the seasoning into a bowl and beat it with a wooden spoon. Put the oil into a bottle with a spout, so that you can drip it out in minute drops. Start adding the oil to the egg yolk a few drops at a time, beating continuously. When the mixture starts to thicken, add a few drops of vinegar or lemon juice, then continue trickling in the oil, adding a little more at a time as it gets thicker, until you are pouring it in a thin thread-like stream, and stirring all the time. Add more vinegar or lemon as necessary. If the egg yolk is small it may not take quarter of a pint of oil; when threads of oil appear in the lines left by the fork or spoon, be very cautious about adding more or it may curdle. When it is finished it can be thinned with cream, top of the milk or warm water to make a pouring consistency for egg mayonnaise etc. If you do curdle your mayonnaise, break a fresh egg yolk into a separate bowl, beat it, and add the curdled lot, a little at a time, until it is all worked in.

For 2–3

GREEN MAYONNAISE

4 pint very thick mayonnaise (this page)
handful of young spinach leaves
handful of watercress
4–5 sprigs parsley
fresh tarragon if available

Blanch all the greenety for two or three minutes in boiling salted water. Squeeze dry and pulverize. You should now have a dark green puree. Put it in a fine sieve to drain the water off.

Just before serving stir it carefully into the mayonnaise. It makes the most beautiful speckled, pale green sauce.

Use instead of plain mayonnaise; it is more special because it looks so marvellous, especially with cold fish and hard-boiled eggs.

MUSTARD SAUCE (1)

¼ pint Hollandaise sauce (opposite)
1–2 teaspoons made English mustard

Make the Hollandaise and when finished stir in one or two teaspoons freshly made mustard.

For 2

MUSTARD SAUCE (2)

¼ pint double cream
teaspoon made mustard
salt and freshly ground pepper

Mix the ingredients together and pour over open filleted cooked fish.

Mustard sauces are marvellous with fried or grilled herring, mackerel or sprats, and with tongue.

For 4

MINT SAUCE

¼ pint wine vinegar
1½ oz Demerara sugar
1 tablespoon finely chopped mint

Bring the vinegar to the boil in a small pan, and dissolve the Demerara sugar in it. Put the mint in a bowl and pour on the boiling vinegar. Allow it to cool.

For lamb.

PIZZAIOLA SAUCE

1 lb tomatoes, fresh or tinned, skinned and chopped
2 tablespoons oil
1 clove garlic, sliced
salt, pepper and a pinch of sugar
handful of parsley, chopped
½ handful of fresh basil or oregano, chopped

Heat the oil in a small frying pan and brown the garlic. Add the tomatoes, salt, pepper and sugar and cook, stirring, for 10–15 minutes. Add the freshly chopped herbs and serve.

For fish, pasta, steaks, chops, kebabs.

SAUCE SOUBISE (ONION SAUCE)

½ lb onions
2 tablespoons butter
2 tablespoons flour
½ pint creamy milk or light, good stock
salt, pepper and nutmeg
pinch of sugar

Peel and slice the onions finely and stew them gently in the butter in a saucepan for 10–15 minutes. They must not brown. Stir in the flour, cook for one minute, then gradually add the heated milk or stock, stirring as it thickens. Season and simmer for 15–20 minutes taking care not to let the sauce catch at the bottom. Sieve or liquidise the mixture, taste for seasoning and sugar and serve hot.

For roast lamb and lamb chops, and for Oeufs à la Tripe (page 41).

ROUILLE

2 red pimentos, bottled or tinned will do
4 cloves garlic, peeled
1 slice white bread, crusts removed
salt to taste
2 tablespoons olive oil
2 tablespoons broth from the fish soup (page 65)

Cut up the peppers, remove the seeds and pound them with the garlic and crumbled bread and a little salt. Gradually add the oil and broth until you have a smooth sauce. It is hot because of the quantity of garlic, so if your cloves are very small use more.

For fish soup or boiled fish.

RED SAUCE

2 tablespoons fresh white breadcrumbs
2 tablespoons wine vinegar
2 cloves garlic
2 large ripe tomatoes, skinned and de-seeded (page 132)
large pinch salt and paprika
6 tablespoons olive oil

Soak the breadcrumbs in the vinegar. Pound the garlic in a mortar and add the tomatoes and breadcrumbs. Season with salt and paprika and add the olive oil gradually, until the sauce is thick.

This is a Spanish sauce whose ingredients sound unlikely, but it is delicious, especially with cold fish or shellfish, hard-boiled eggs, or with a plain potato salad instead of dressing or mayonnaise.

For 4

SAUCE BEARNAISE

4 tablespoons wine vinegar
1 shallot
1 bayleaf
1 blade of mace
6 peppercorns
2 large egg yolks
4 oz fresh butter
1 heaped teaspoon of chopped tarragon, chervil and parsley, mixed
salt and freshly ground pepper

Reduce the vinegar with the spices to a tablespoon. Work the yolks with a nut of the softened butter, strain the vinegar over them, stir and thicken in a bain-marie, gradually adding the rest of the butter stirring constantly. Add the herbs and seasoning.

For grilled fish or meat.

CUMBERLAND SAUCE

4 oranges
2 lemons
2 small shallots
1 dessertspoon fresh English or Dijon mustard
3 tablespoons cheap wine or wine vinegar
1 large glass cheap port
1 lb redcurrant jelly
salt and freshly ground pepper

Peel the oranges and lemons very thinly with a potato peeler, so that the pieces of peel have no pith. Cut the peel into tiny thin strips, cover them with cold water in a small pan, bring to the boil and then strain immediately. Peel and chop the shallots very finely, put in a small pan, cover with cold water, boil for a few minutes and strain. Mix the mustard, wine, port and the juice of the lemons and of two of the oranges. (Use more orange juice if they aren't very juicy). Stir in the redcurrant jelly and dissolve it slowly over a low heat. Add the peel and shallots and a generous seasoning of salt and pepper. Simmer 20 minutes or more until it thickens a bit, pour into small jars and keep in the fridge. It keeps a week or two and has a very sweet spicy flavour.

For cold ham, duck, turkey or game.

CHILLI TOMATO SAUCE

1 onion, finely chopped
2 red chilli peppers or 1 teaspoon chilli powder (more if liked)
1 lb tomatoes, skinned and chopped
3–4 cloves garlic, peeled and chopped finely
salt and freshly ground pepper
thyme, sage and parsley tied in a bunch
butter and oil

Heat a little butter and oil in a frying pan, add the onions and soften them. Stir in the chillies or chilli powder, fry for a minute or two and then add the tomatoes, garlic, seasoning and herbs.

Simmer uncovered until you have a thickish sauce, remove the herbs and sieve or liquidise.

Reheat in the same pan before serving. This can be ferociously or gently hot according to how much chilli you put in.

A hot sauce, excellent with fried chicken.

TOMATO SAUCE

2 onions
2 cloves garlic
2 tablespoons olive oil
1½ lbs tomatoes
½ glass red wine
sprigs of thyme and rosemary and a bayleaf
salt and freshly ground pepper

Chop the onions and garlic finely and soften them in the oil in a saucepan for about ten minutes without browning. Add the skinned roughly chopped tomatoes, seasoning, red wine and bundle of herbs. Simmer 45 minutes, uncovered.

For pasta, fried fish etc.

For 6

VINAIGRETTE

4–5 tablespoons oil
4 teaspoon sea salt
several pinches freshly ground black pepper
1 teaspoon white sugar (optional)
2 teaspoons wine vinegar

Take a small bowl, mix the salt, pepper and sugar and add the oil. Then stir in the vinegar with a teaspoon; it should become thick and cloudy. Pour it over your green salad just as your serve it, and turn the leaves over until they glisten with oil. If you like garlic add a clove, first thoroughly pulverised with the salt, using the point of a stainless kitchen knife. If you only quite like it, put a few cubes of dried bread or rusk, thoroughly rubbed with cut cloves of garlic, into the bottom of the salad bowl.

If you like a thick mustardy dressing, mix the vinegar with half a teaspoon of Dijon mustard and season this, leaving out the sugar, before you gradually add the oil.

For salads and cold vegetables.

VINAIGRETTE A L'OEUF

vinaigrette (above)
1 small onion or shallot chopped finely
a few chives, chopped
1 soft-boiled egg

Add the onion, chives and the yolk of the soft-boiled egg to the vinaigrette. Chop the white and add this too.

Good with boiled fowl or fish.

HERB BUTTERS

These all make good fresh herb butters:

Mint: ideal for lamb, peas, new potatoes.

Parsley: for steak, fish or broad beans.

Tarragon: for potatoes, chicken or eggs.

Chives and parsley together: for steak, fish, lamb chops.

Rosemary: for lamb, pork, chicken, haricot beans.

Savory or Thyme: for grilled kidneys etc.

If you have a special chopping-bowl or a Mouli-Parsmint, chop the herbs in it, otherwise chop as finely as possible with a knife. Don't use more than one or two herbs, fresh and in generous amounts.

For each person chop about one heaped teaspoon of herbs and mash it with a walnut of butter, a squeeze of lemon, salt and fresh ground pepper. Form into a one-inch roll in a piece of greaseproof paper, and put into the refrigerator to become firm. Place a half-inch slice of the roll on the food as you serve it.

Herb butters keep for up to a week in the refrigerator.

For serving with vegetables or grilled fish or meat.

PUDDINGS

This chapter concentrates mainly on puddings that children like, since many people now seem to want to go straight on to fresh fruit and cheese; but if your first course is nothing much, then a good pudding does help to salvage your reputation.

One or two steamed puddings are included, and although they are a bit of a challenge to the modem stomach, they are comforting on a cold winter's day after a morning in the fresh air.

Vanilla sugar is mentioned in several recipes; this is made by putting a vanilla pod into an airtight glass storage jar, and filling it up with caster sugar. Let it stay there, refilling with sugar when necessary, until it loses its aroma, which is only after several months. The flavour given by vanilla sugar is different and much better than the flavour of vanilla essence.

RICH SWEET FLAN PASTRY

6 oz plain flour
2 oz slightly salted butter
2 oz cooking fat
1 oz granulated sugar
1 egg yolk
a few drops cold water
pinch of salt

Sieve the flour and salt into a mixing bowL Chop the butter and fat into small pieces in the flour.

Add the sugar and rub it all together very lightly with your finger tips until it is integrated. Blend in the egg yolk, using a knife, and then add just a few drops of water to make it the consistency of soft, light marzipan.

Leave it in a cool place wrapped in greaseproof paper, cloth, or polythene for at least three-quarters of an hour.

TO MAKE AND BAKE A FRUIT FLAN

Preheat the oven to Reg 5½/200°. Press the pastry into an eight-inch loose flan ring, previously buttered, on a baking sheet, also buttered. It is too crumbly and sticky to roll out. Arrange the fruit (sliced apples or halved stoned apricots or plums) prettily in the flan. Sprinkle with sugar and bake ten minutes. Then lower heat and bake another 20 minutes at Reg 4/180°. Allow to shrink and cool before sliding away the ring and lifting the tart with excruciating care on to a plate or dish,. Glaze the top with syrup from in between the fruit, or with melted apricot jam.

See also page Making Flan cases (page 172)

BAKED APPLE DUMPLINGS

4 medium-sized apples, peeled and cored
½ oz butter
1 oz Demerara sugar
1 teaspoon grated lemon rind (optional)
for the pastry:
½ lb flour
2 oz butter
2 oz cooking fat pinch of salt
water to mix

Make the pastry and let it stand in a coal place for at least half an hour. Preheat the oven to Reg 5/190° Peel and core the apples; mash the butter, sugar, and lemon rind, and stuff the apples with the mixture. Divide the pastry into four and roll out into four thin circles on a floured board. Place an apple on the centre of each; damp the edges and neatly bring the pastry up round each apple, pinching it together and trimming off any excess. Place the apples, joined side down, on a greased baking sheet, decorate the tops with pastry leaves and stalks, brush with water and sprinkle generously. with caster sugar.

Bake the apples for 30 minutes and serve hot with cream.

For 4

APPLE CRUMBLE (OR APRICOT, OR BLACKBERRY AND APPLE)

1½ lbs cooking apples or apricots or 1½ lbs blackberries and apples
sugar to sweeten the fruit
2 oz soft brown sugar
2 oz butter
4 oz plain flour
pinch of cinnamon

Preheat the oven to Reg 3/160°. Put the prepared fruit into a casserole with enough sugar to sweeten, cover and stew gently in the oven until the juice begins to run, or the apples begin to soften in 20–30 minutes.

Meanwhile rub the flour, butter, sugar and cinnamon together until the mixture looks like breadcrumbs. Take the fruit out of the oven, turn the oven up to Reg 6/200° and sprinkle the crumble mixture over the fruit. Return to the oven, uncovered, for 20 minutes, or until crisp and golden on top.

Serve hot with cream.

For 4

APPLE FLAN

2 lbs dessert apples (Golden Delicious are best)
½ small teaspoon powdered cinnamon
2 tablespoons brown sugar
2 tablespoons red wine vinegar
1 lb shortcrust pastry (page 172)

Preheat oven to Reg 5½/200°. Peel and slice the apples, and put them in a pan with the cinnamon, sugar and vinegar. Simmer covered, stirring occasionally, for half an hour; allow to cool. Line a seven-inch flan tin with a moveable base with two-thirds of the pastry. Fill with the apple mixture and cover with two-thirds of the remaining pastry. Decorate the top with a huge flower and bake in a moderate oven, Reg 5½/200°, for 30 minutes. Cover the top with sifted sugar when the pie has slightly cooled. The apples will be a wonderful golden brown and very spicy, and the vinegar flavour so delicate you could hardly tell.

For 5

APPLE FRITTERS

4 apples
fritter batter (page 56)
ground cinnamon and cloves
caster sugar

Peel and core the apples and cut in rings. Press them with the sugar, mixed with the cinnamon and cloves, and then dip them into the batter. Deep-fry in hot oil and drain on kitchen paper. Sprinkle with caster sugar. They are best served at once but can be kept warm in a low oven.

Cook banana or pineapple slices the same way.

For 4–5

FRIED BANANAS

6 bananas, peeled and halved lengthwise
1½ oz butter
juice of half a lemon
Demerara sugar
1 tablespoon brandy, rum or liqueur
single cream

Melt the butter in a large frying pan; as it foams put in the bananas. Brown them gently on each side for a few minutes, add the lemon juice and let it sizzle. Warm a spoonful of brandy or whatever, set light to it and pour, flaming, over the bananas. Sprinkle with Demerara sugar and serve at once, with cream if liked.

For 4

BANANA SOUFFLE

4 bananas
2 whole eggs, plus 2 whites
dash of rum
1 oz butter
1½ oz flour
½ pint milk
2 oz vanilla sugar

Butter a two-pint souffle dish. Put three of the bananas in their skins into a moderate oven, Reg 4/180°, for about ten minutes, while you make a sauce with the butter, flour, milk and sugar. Remove the bananas and turn up the oven to Reg 7/220°.

While the sauce cools prepare the bananas by removing the skins, which have gone black, and pulping the fruit. Stir them into the sauce, and add the egg yolks and the rum, stirring all the time. Cut the remaining banana into cubes and stir it in. Beat the egg whites to a firm snow and fold them into the sauce. Turn the mixture into the buttered souffle dish, put it in the oven, turn down the heat to Reg 6/200° and cook for half an hour. Serve at once dusted with fine sugar.

For 4

BATTER PUDDING

Batter (page 56)
2 tablespoons butter, lard or oil
4 oz raisins, sultanas or currants, or all three mixed
golden syrup and cream

Make the batter two hours before you need it. Preheat the oven to Reg 9/240°. Put two tablespoons of fat in a baking tin and heat in the oven for a few minutes. Stir the washed, thoroughly dirained and dried fruit into the batter, pour it into the very hot fat and return it to the oven. After five minutes lower the heat to Reg 6/200°, and cook 35–40 minutes.

Serve hot with warmed treacle and top of the milk or cream.

For 4–6

BREAD AND BUTTER PUDDING

6 slices assorted bread and butter (white, brown or currant loaf, or a mixture of all three)
handful of currants, raisins or sultanas
2 eggs
1 tablespoon sugar (preferably vanilla)
¾–1 pint milk

Lay the bread, crusts cut off, in a buttered pie dish in layers, with fruit in between. Beat the eggs with the sugar and add the milk. Pour over the bread and leave to soak for half an hour or so. Cook in a low oven, Reg 1/140°, for one hour, loosely covered with greaseproof paper and for a further half hour, uncovered, to puff and brown.

For 4

COMPOTE OF FRUIT

1 lb washed fresh fruit
½ pint water
4 oz sugar

Heat the sugar and water in a saucepan and when the sugar has dissolved bring it to the boil and carefully put in the fruit. It will not be covered by the liquid so turn it over gently once or twice to coat it. Return to the boil and then turn the heat down as low as it will go, and cover the pan. Leave for ten minutes for soft fruit, 15 minutes or more for apples and pears; the fruit should be tender but still whole. Remove it carefully with a perforated spoon and put it in a glass or china bowl. Return the liquid to the heat and boil, uncovered, to a thickish syrup. Allow to cool, then pour it over the fruit.

Use plums, greengages, apricots, Morello cherries, peeled pears or apples, quartered or sliced.

For 4

CLAFOUTIS

2 eggs
3 oz sugar
1½ oz flour
¼ pint double cream
½ pint milk
1 lb stoned black cherries
kirsch (optional)

Preheat oven to Reg 5/190°. Cream the eggs and sugar in a basin, beating hard with an electric beater or wire whisk. Add the flour all at once, beat it in and add the cream, then the milk. Put the cherries in a shallow earthenware oven dish, pour over the batter and cook in the oven for 35 minutes. The batter should be brown on top and halfway between custard and cake inside. Eat it hot or cold with cream.

This is really delicious but can be improved slightly by the addition of a tiny glass of Kirsch just before the cream. The whole thing is rather indigestible but worth it.

You can me otherfruit such as plums, apples and apricots, which are cheaper and mare often available.

For 4–6

EGG CUSTARD

1 large egg
2 tablespoons vanilla sugar
½ pint milk

Mix the egg and sugar in a basin. Heat the milk to scalding point (almost boiling but not quite), pour it on to the egg, whisking as you do so.

Return the mixture to the milk pan and heat gradually, without boiling of course, over a low heat, stirring constantly with a wooden spoon. When it has thickened enough to coat the spoon, take it off the heat.

For steamed and other puddings.

JULIA'S RICE PUDDING

2 level tablespoons pudding rice
1 level tablespoon vanilla sugar, or plain sugar and vanilla essence
pinch salt
few chips lemon peel
1 teaspoon butter
1 pint milk

Put the oven on the lowest possible heat. Take a saucepan and put in the milk, sugar, salt and lemon peel. Bring to the boil while you butter a one-pint pudding dish or pie dish. Turn the boiling milk and rice into the dish and leave it, uncovered, in your low,

low oven for five hours. Remove the black skin before eating a really good, creamy, succulent dish of mother's favourite pudding. Eat it with cream and sugar.

For those who enjoy the skin keep the pudding covered for the first four hours, then allow to brown.

For 4–5

BLACKBERRY WATER ICE

1 lb raw blackberries
4 oz sugar
¼ pint water
1 small egg white

Turn the refrigerator to its coldest setting. Make a syrup by boiling the sugar and water for four minutes. Allow it to cool. Sieve or mouli the blackberries and mix with the syrup. Beat the egg white until it forms soft peaks and fold thoroughly into the blackberry mixture.

Put into a dish, cover and freeze to a mush. Stir and freeze for a further half hour. Stir again and freeze until set, about 2½–3 hours altogether.

This can also be made with raspberries or loganberries.

For 4

COFFEE GRANITA

4 oz vanilla sugar
¾ pint hot, double strength coffee

Dissolve the sugar in the coffee, pour the mixture into the ice-making tray and freeze until mushy. Remove it to a bowl and beat with a fork. Return and freeze to sorbet consistency. Serve in glasses with a dollop of cream if you like.

For 4

LEMON ICE

8 oz sugar
juice of 2 lemons
grated rind of 1 lemon
1½ pint milk
2 teaspoons gelatine crystals melted in 2 tablespoons water

Dissolve the sugar in the lemon juice. Add the milk and gelatine, stirring well. Add the finely grated rind of one lemon and freeze, covered, in the ice compartment of your refrigerator, turned to its coldest setting, for three hours. Stir the mixture twice during the setting time.

For 6

GRAPEFRUIT SHERBET

12 oz caster sugar
2 large grapefruit
¾ pint water
squeeze lemon juice
2 egg whites
tiny pinch salt

Stir the sugar and the finely grated rind of one of the grapefruit into the water in a thick saucepan, Heat gradually, stirring; when the sugar has dissolved, bring the mixture to the boil and boil fast for five minutes. Allow to cool, stir in the juice of the two grapefruits and a squeeze of lemon juice, and put in the freezer tray in the refrigerator; freeze to a mush.

Beat the egg whites to soft peaks with a little pinch of salt; fold them into the mush and freeze at the coldest setting on the refrigerator for half an hour. Whip until the egg whites are spread evenly through the mixture and freeze again for 2½–3 hours.

For 8

CARAMELISED ORANGES

4 oranges
4 oz caster sugar
water

Peel the oranges over a plate with a very sharp knife, removing the peel and pithy skin at the same time. Slice carefully on the plate into thin slices, cut these in half, removing the pips and centre core.

Lay them on a dish like the scales of a fish. Caramelise the sugar with the orange juice collected on the plate and a couple of tablespoons of water. When the sugar turns golden brown watch it carefully darken to deep chestnut, then pour it in a thin layer over the sliced oranges.

Don't make this too far ahead of time because the caramel will lose its crispness.

For 4

CANDIED ORANGES

6 large juicy seedless oranges
½ pint water
6 oz granulated sugar
liqueur (optional)

Use a very sharp stainless steel knife with a saw-edge to score each orange with long narrow cuts forming strips running from top to bottom of the fruit. Then peel these off with your knife, or a sharp potato peeler, as thinly as you can so that you have a heap of little pithless orange-peel matchsticks.

If you like a bland rather than a slightly bitter flavour, blanch the strips for one minute in boiling water and drain them well. Melt the sugar in the water and bring to the boil; poach the orange-peel strips in this syrup, uncovered, until tender, about 15 minutes.

Put the oranges, stripped of every shred of pith and skin, on a dish, and pour the syrup over them; allow to cool. Arrange the shreds of peel in little mounds on top of each one. Every Italian restaurant seems to have these on the sweet trolley and they are always refreshing and delicious.

You can add a liqueur such as Grand Marnier to the syrup if you want.

For 6

ORANGE FRITTERS

Fritter batter (page 56)
2 large oranges, seedless if possible
deep oil for frying
caster sugar

Peel the oranges very carefully, removing all the white pith, but don't cut into the orange at all. Break into pieces of two or three segments. Dip each piece into the batter and fry in hot oil until golden brown. Serve sprinkled with more sugar.

For 4

ORANGE JELLIES

6 large oranges
1 packet orange jelly (to make 1 pint)

Cut the oranges across in halves and squeeze the juice into a jug. Strain and measure it and use it, made up with enough water, to make the orange jelly. Remove all the skin and pith from inside the orange halves so that each one makes a clean bowl, and pour in the hot, dissolved jelly. Leave to set, and when quite firm you can cut each half in two, so they look like orange slices miraculously made of jelly.

This is pure children's party food.

For 6–12 children, depending on their size

SWEET PANCAKES

½ lb plain flour
¾ pint milk and water, half and half
1 large or 2 small eggs
1 tablespoon melted butter or oil
1 tablespoon sugar
¼ teaspoon salt

Make the pancake batter at least two hours before using it, as the starch granules need time to expand and absorb the liquid to make a really good pancake.Put the sifted flour in a large mixing bowl, make a well in the centre and gradually add the milk and water, working the flour in with a wooden spoon.

When all the flour is smoothly incorporated into the liquid, add the beaten eggs, melted butter or oil, sugar and salt, and beat the mixture thoroughly. It should have the consistency of thin cream. Add more milk if necessary, and then let it stand.

Have ready:

a frying pan
4 oz lard, cut into cubes the size of a sugar lump
a coffee cup
a large pan of hot water covered with a plate
a dozen strips of greaseproof paper, 1 inch wide, and 3 inches longer than the diameter of the pan

The painstaking preparations make the cooking of the pancakes much faster and easier, so do not despair.

Heat the frying pan on a brisk heat, drop a lump of lard into it, and tip the pan from side to side so that the base is coated. Stir the batter and fill the coffee cup. Tilt the pan and pour the batter in at the highest point, rotating the pan to cover the base completely with a very thin layer of batter. It should set at once. Let it cook until it shifts when you shake the pan, then flip it over with a spatula, first making sure it is not sticking anywhere. Cook the other side, and slip the pancake on to the plate

over the pan of hot water. Put a strip of paper across and continue cooking the pancakes and piling them up, with strips of paper in between, to prevent them from sticking together.

The pancakes are now ready to be filled 6r sprinkled with lemon and sugar. Experts flip the pancakes into the air to turn them and keep two pans going at once.

For 12–14 average pancakes

ORANGE PANCAKES

8 thin pancakes, freshly made (opposite)
2 oranges
2 oz granulated sugar
4 oz butter

Grate oranges finely all over and mix the peel with the sugar. Soften the butter and beat the sugar into it, gradually adding the juice of the oranges. This butter can then be wrapped and chilled in the refrigerator until you need it; it keeps several days.

Put the orange butter in a frying pan over a moderate heat. When it starts to bubble lay a pancake in the pan, spoon the butter over it and then fold in it half and half again with a palette knife. Put the folded, juicy pancake on a hot dish, and put another one into the slowly bubbling sauce. Repeat the spooning and folding process until all the pancakes are used up; pour any extra butter over the folded parcels of pancake and serve immediately. You can also make this with lemons, using more sugar.

For 4

SWEET PANCAKES WITH CREAM CHEESE

12 freshly made very thin pancakes (opposite)
8 oz cream cheese
1 egg yolk
2 oz caster sugar
2 oz raisins
2 oz chopped blanched almonds
1–2 oz butter

Put the cream cheese, beaten egg yolk and sugar in a bowl and beat together with a fork. Add the raisins and nuts and stir them in. Put a large dollop of the mixture in a strip in the middle of each pancake, and fold it over as if you were wrapping a parcel.

Heat the butter in the frying pan, drop in the little parcels, brown them all over and serve hot, sprinkled with caster sugar. You can serve cream with these.

These are very filling.

For 6

FROSTED REDCURRANTS (1)

1 lb redcurrants on their stems
4 oz granulated sugar
½ pint water
caster sugar

Carefully pick over and wash the currants if you are not sure they are clean. Shake off all the water. Make a syrup by boiling the granulated sugar with water for five minutes. Keeping the syrup gently on the boil, dip the branches of redcurrants first into the syrup, shaking off th^ extra drips, then into the caster sugar, shaking again. Then put them on a large flat dish covered with a white paper doily. It is easy if the currants are held by the end of the stalk or hooked on to the prongs of a fork, but they must only be dipped into the syrup for a moment and flicked in and out of the caster sugar. Lay them out side by side and let them harden as they dry – drying in the sun is ideal. They can be kept in the refrigerator until they are needed. Children adore them and they make a lovely end to a summer dinner party. It is rather fiddly and takes a long time but is still rather fun to do.

FROSTED REDCURRANTS (2)

These are made as before but dipped into whipped egg whites instead of hot syrup. Turn them over from time to time as they dry. This is good if the currants are very ripe, but shop ones tend to be on the unripe side and less sweet as a result.

Serve ice-cold. Lovely to make on a fine summer's day.

For 6

RICOTTA WITH COFFEE

4 oz Ricotta (or cottage cheese)
2 tablespoons freshly ground coffee
1 teaspoon caster sugar
Cream (optional)

Sprinkle each person's helping of cheese with the sugar and ground coffee. That's all. Serve with cream if you have some.

For 2

STRAWBERRY FOOL

½ pint double cream, as cold as possible
1 lb second-rate strawberries
6 oz caster sugar

Whisk the cream until it is softly thick, and gradually add five ounces of caster sugar. Whisk on until the cream stands in peaks, but is still soft; over-beating leaves you with a bowl full of butter.

Hull the strawberries, leaving a few of the best ones for decoration afterwards. Mash them to a pulp, the potato masher does this quickly, and add an ounce of caster sugar.

Fold the puree into the cream so that it is not really well mixed, and tip the whole thing into a pretty bowl or glass dish. Put the strawberries you kept for best on top and chill in the refrigerator.

This can be made just as well with raspberries. It is one of the great luxuries of high summer, both delicate and rich, and of a beautiful soft pink. It sounds extravagant but a little of it goes a long way, far further than plain strawberries and cream, and it makes use of fruit that may be past its best, which you could not eat whole.

For 5–6

SUMMER PUDDING

1 lb raspberries
½ lb redcurrants
½ lb blackcurrants
6–8 oz caster sugar
several slices white bread

Cook each kind of fruit separately with a few tablespoons of sugar and one tablespoon of water, to stop them catching on the pan before the juice starts to run out. They should be cooked as briefly as possible, the raspberries scarcely at all. Line a seven-inch pudding basin with medium slices of white bread, crusts removed, cutting them into wedge shapes to fit the sides of the bowl. Put in the redcurrants first, then the blackcurrants for the second layer and finally the raspberries, using all the fruit juice. On top put a layer of slices of bread (crusts removed as before), and cover with a saucer, slightly smaller in diameter than the pudding bowl. Place weights, which could be put inside a polythene bag in case the juice comes up over the top of the saucer, on the saucer.

Leave overnight in the refrigerator and turn out carefully the following day.

This should be made the day before you want it.

For 4–6

ROLY POLY PUDDING

½ lb flour, self-raising, or plain with 3 teaspoons baking powder
5 oz shredded suet
pinch salt
2 tablespoons sugar
water
1 pot of jam
1 large doubled square of butter muslin, or a thick clean tea-towel, scalded and thickly floured
6 pins

Put a large pan of water on to boil. Make a suet pastry by mixing the flour, suet, salt and sugar with a knife and adding enough water to make a stiff dough. Roll it out on the floured cloth so that it forms a rectangle about 9 x 18 inches. Spread jam or treacle thickly down the middle, leaving a margin of about two inches at the sides and at one end. Brush the margin with cold water, then roll up the pastry lightly, as if making a Swiss roll, starting at the jammy end. Squeeze the ends together firmly and pat the join to seal it.

Roll the cloth loosely round the pudding, allowing for it to swell in cooking. Pin the side and ends, and fold the ends to form a handle. Drop the pudding into boiling water (it should float) and boil, covered, for two hours. Add more boiling water from time to time. Carefully remove the cloth and all the pins, and serve with hot jam.

Instead of spreading the pastry with jam you can cover it with a layer of currants and raisins (Spotted Dick), or stoned chopped dates, or with chopped rhubarb or apple, or stoned plums.

For 6

TREACLE SPONGE

4 oz butter, 4 oz sugar
2 eggs, beaten
teaspoon grated lemon rind
5 oz self-raising flour
pinch of salt, milk to mix
For top of pudding:
3 tablespoons golden syrup
juice of 4 lemon
½ teaspoon caraway seeds
small handful breadcrumbs

Mix the syrup, lemon juice, c naraway seeds and breadcrumbs in the bottom of a buttered two-pint pudding basin. Cream the butter and sugar together until fluffy, add the beaten eggs and the lemon rind and then the flour with a pinch of salt. Add a little milk to bring the mixture to a dropping consistency. Turn it into the basin, on top of the treacle and lemon juice mixture, cover well with a double layer of greased greaseproof paper and a cloth, or double aluminium foil, and steam for two hours, covered, in a large pan of water.

Serve, turned out, with more golden syrup, warmed, and cream if there is some available.

For 6

SIX-CUP PUDDING

Use an ordinary teacup that contains half a pint
1 cup sugar
1 cup butter (7 oz)
1 beaten egg
1 cup raisins
1 cup currants
1 cup self-raising flour, or 1 cup plain flour and ½ teaspoon baking powder
1 teaspoon mixed spice
1 cup milk

Cream the sugar and butter together, add the egg, fruit, and then the flour, baking powder and spice. Moisten with milk, beating the mixture until it drops off the spoon. You may not need all the milk. Turn it into a greased basin, cover and steam for hours.

Serve this with home-made custard (page 150) for a very good, thoroughly British, rib-sticking pudding.

For 6–8

TREACLE TART

4 oz fresh brown breadcrumbs
1 cup golden syrup
For pastry:
6 oz self-raising flour
3 oz cooking fat
pinch salt
water to mix

Make the pastry and let it stand in a cool place for at least half an hour. Preheat the oven to Reg 6/200°. Grease an eight-inch flan tin and line it with the pastry. Fill with breadcrumbs and pour the syrup over generously. Use the pastry trimmings to make a slender lattice over the syrup. Bake for 20–30 minutes and eat hot.

For 4–6

TOFFEE SAUCE

1 oz butter
3 oz brown sugar
2 tablespoons golden syrup
4 tablespoons cream

Put all the ingredients in a small saucepan and heat together gently until hot and melted, but not boiling. Serve hot.

For vanilla ice cream.

CAKES, BISCUITS AND BREAD

Like suet puddings, huge great teas at tables spread with homemade cakes and scones and biscuits seem to be vanishing (much to the consternation of the people who make and sell flour). Children's teas now seem to be a form of supper, and after a ham salad or a hamburger it is hard to be enthusiastic about a many-layered chocolate gateau. It is at weekends, especially if you come from the North, and are not on an almost perpetual diet, that all the delicious buns and tea-breads can be tried, and it makes a very cosy sight. You feel like a genuine mother or wife if there are home-made things for tea, and they are cheaper than bought ones, and contain only ingredients you have chosen yourself.

These recipes are all of a simple straightforward nature; there are no flights into the realms of mille-feuilles and sachertorte because the authors have never had time to get really familiar with the making of them, and feel it is better to leave the subject to those who love cake-making.

In all cakes and biscuits margarine can be used instead of butter; it is slightly cheaper and it creams faster, but the end products do lose a little in flavour.

If you want to bake your own bread it would be hard to find a recipe better than Elizabeth David's English Loaf, which uses no sugar and no fat in the making and is the most delicious straightforward loaf of bread imaginable. If you have difficulty in finding fresh yeast (it should be available through any baker that bakes his own bread, and most health food shops) try using freshly-bought dried yeast, giving it plenty of time to get working before you add it to your flour mixture. It likes a few grains of sugar to feed on, but does not need as much as is recommended on the packet, since using that amount might spoil the plain nature of the bread. Always buy special bread flour to make a loaf; ordinary commercial flour is finely milled specially for the making of pastry, cakes and so on, and is not good for bread. If you can find unbleached white flour it makes a loaf with a very good flavour.

PLAIN SPONGE CAKE

4 oz caster sugar
4 oz unsalted butter
4 oz self-raising flour, or 4 oz plain flour plus 1½ teaspoons baking powder
2 eggs

Preheat the oven to Reg 5/190°. Butter and flour two eight-inch sandwich tins. Cream the sugar and butter together and when white and fluffy add the well-beaten eggs, a little at a time. Fold in the sifted flour thoroughly.

Spread half the mixture in each tin as lightly as you can, spreading it to the sides with a palette knife so that the finished cake will be flat rather than domed.

Bake in the top half of the oven for 15–20 minutes. Do not open the oven while the cakes are cooking or they may go sad. When they are cooked take them out and cool on a wire rack. Spread one half with whipped cream and the other with jam. Press the halves together so jam and cream are both in the middle.

QUICK SPONGE CAKE

4 oz soft margarine
4 oz caster sugar
2 eggs
4 oz self-raising flour
1 level teaspoon baking powder

Preheat the oven to Reg 5/190°. Butter and flour two seven-inch Victoria sponge tins.

Sieve everything into a bowl and beat at top speed for 40 seconds. Turn the mixture into the prepared tins, flatten the top with a palette knife and bake for 15–20 minutes. Fill the middle with raspberry jam and cream, and sprinkle the top with sugar.

If the mixture is ready before the oven is up to full heat, put it in the refrigerator to check the action of the raising agent.

This mixture takes about 40 seconds to make with an electric beater. Don't be tempted to give it longer as overbeating toughens the cake. The trick is to use one of the specially soft margarines, which won't go solid even in the refrigerator .

The sponge is made and cooked in less than half an hour

MADELEINES

2 eggs and their weight in:
caster sugar (vanilla sugar if possible)
unsalted butter, softened
self-raising flour
juice of ½ lemon

Preheat the oven to Reg 5/190°. Separate the egg yolks from the whites. Beat the yolks and sugar together in a basin until white and fluffy. Add the butter softened to a creamy consistency, and beat away until the mixture is smooth. Beat in the flour, and lemon juice and finally the egg whites, broken up with a fork but not beaten. Butter the Madeleine tins which have shell-shaped indentations, or shallow jam tart tins and put a spoonful of the mixture, about the size of a walnut, in each well. Bake in the centre of the oven for 15-20 minutes. Beware – they can go from not cooked to burned in a very short time. They should be brown round the edges.

Eat them the same day if you can; they are very crisp outside, light and soft inside.

Makes 24–30

CAROLINA BISCUITS

½ lb margarine
6 oz pale soft brown sugar
1 egg white
1–2 teaspoons cinnamon
1 teaspoon ground ginger
pinch salt
10 oz flour

Preheat the oven to Reg 5/190° and grease two baking sheets. Beat the margarine with the sugar, egg white, spices and pinch of salt, using a wire whisk or electric beater. When it is thoroughly creamed add the flour and beat it in. Spread the mixture thinly on baking sheets with a spatula and bake 10–15 minutes to a nice golden brown. The mixture may seem very wet before cooking; spread it on the tins with well-floured hands if this is easier.

Cut the mixture in diamond shapes while it is hot. These biscuits should be thin, fragile and spicy.

Makes about 48

PLAIN BISCUIT MIXTURE

4 oz unsalted butter
4 oz caster sugar
8 oz plain flour
1 small egg

Cream the sugar and butter together, add the beaten egg, stir in the sifted flour, mix to a firm dough. Ideally leave it to rest in the refrigerator, but if in a hurry carry on. Set the oven to Reg 5/190°. Roll the dough thinly and cut into shapes. At places like Fortnum & Mason they cut them into stars and moons, oak leaves and acorns. Place the shapes in a buttered and floured tin, brushing some with beaten egg, if liked. Put the tin near the top of the oven for ten minutes or until done. Leave to cool and crisp on the tin and then on a wire rack.

Variations: dip half of each biscuit (especially for acorns and oakleaves) into melted chocolate; or cover with white icing, flavoured with vanilla or almond essence.

You can add ginger or vanilla or chopped nuts to the mixture before baking.

This is so easy that children can make it by themselves.

SCOTCH COOKIES

1 egg
4 oz caster sugar
2 oz butter, softened
¼ pint milk
1 lb self-raising flour, or less

Preheat the oven to Reg 7½/225°. Cream the egg and sugar together, add the softened butter, beat it in, mix in the milk and then add enough flour to make the mixture the consistency of pastry. Roll out to quarter-inch thickness on a floured board, cut into two-inch circles with a glass or pastry-cutter and place on a buttered and floured baking-sheet. Bake just above the middle of the oven for 12 minutes; they will rise and go golden brown. Serve warm, sliced in half with butter and jam and cream. Next day they can be halved and toasted. Don't let anybody think that you were really trying to make scones.

This is a sort of hybrid, halfway between a biscuit and a scone.

Makes 24

DERBY SAGE CHEESE STRAWS

6 oz plain flour
salt, pepper, and a pinch cayenne
4 oz butter
1 egg yolk
4 oz finely grated Derby Sage cheese
1 tablespoon water

Preheat the oven to Reg 5/190°. Sift the flour with the seasoning into a mixing bowl, drop in the butter and cut it into the flour. Rub it in lightly and quickly with your fingertips until the mixture looks like breadcrumbs, Add the cheese and stir it in with a knife.

Mix the egg yolk and water, add to the dry ingredients and mix quickly to a firm dough. Knead lightly until smooth and chill for half an hour before rolling it out to about ¼ inch thick. Cut into narrow strips about two inches long. Bake on a lightly greased baking sheet until cooked, 15–20 minutes; they will be a lovely freckled greeny colour.

This recipe is perfectly suitable for Cheddar or Cheshire cheese.

FIVE-MINUTE BALLATER SCONES

8 oz flour, 1 level teaspoon cream of tartar and ½ small teaspoon bicarbonate of soda, or use 8 oz self-raising flour plus a pinch of baking powder
1½ oz butter
¼ teaspoon salt
¼ pint tepid milk (sour is good)

Preheat the oven to Reg 7½/225°. Sieve the flour, cream of tartar, bicarbonate of soda and salt into a bowl. Rub in the butter at top speed, stir in enough milk to make a slightly stiff dough, and knead the mixture lightly in the bowl.

Roll out to half-inch thickness on a floured board and cut into two-inch rounds. Put them on a buttered baking sheet and place them just above the centre of the oven. When they are nicely puffed up and pale golden, after 10–15 minutes, take them out and brush the tops with milk.

Eat them warm.

Makes 12 scones

DROPSCONES

8 oz self-raising flour
½ teaspoon salt
1 oz caster sugar
1 beaten egg
just over ¼ pint milk, preferably sour, or buttermilk
lard to grease the griddle

Heat the griddle. Mix the dry ingredients in a bowl; make a well in the centre and add the egg and half the milk. Stir until the mixture is thick and smooth, then add the rest of the milk gradually, stirring all the time, until it is the consistency of cream. Pour into a jug.

Rub a piece of lard the size of a hazelnut quickly over the hot griddle on the point of a knife. Pour the batter on to the griddle in rounds about two inches across. Fry them till bubbles appear on the surface and the undersides are light brown. Flip them over with a palette knife and brown the other sides.

Add more lard to the griddle and start again. As each batch is finished put it into a folded teatowel to keep soft and warm.

Serve hot with plenty of butter.

Makes 15–20 scones

MIDLOTHIAN OATCAKES

8 oz oatmeal (fine or coarse – porridge oats will do
4 oz flour
½ teaspoon or more salt
1 teaspoon baking powder
water
3 oz butter, or half butter and half lard

Place the oatmeal in a basin. Sift in the flour, salt and baking powder. Rub in the fat and mix to a stiff dough with cold water. Turn the dough on to a board sprinkled with oatmeal, knead lightly and roll out to less than ¼ inch thickness. Cut into rounds with a glass or teacup and bake in a moderate oven, Reg 4/180°, for 25 minutes. They should not brown, or only very slightly.

Eat with butter for tea; they are also very good with cheese, at the end of a meal.

Makes about 20

MOYNA'S IRISH BREAD

9 heaped tablespoons wholewheat flour (½ lb)
2 heaped tablespoons plain flour
1 level teaspoon brown sugar
1 heaped teaspoon salt
1 heaped teaspoon baking powder
½ pint sour milk or buttermilk

Preheat the oven to Reg 8½/235°. Mix the dry ingredients in a bowl; add enough sour milk to make a soft dough. It may take less than half a pint. Turn the mixture into a buttered and floured bread tin and bake 35-40 minutes. When it is cooked wrap it in a clean, damp tea-cloth and put it on a wire rack to cool. This prevents the crust from becoming too crumbly. If you have not got any sour milk, add a little lemon juice to some fresh milk and stir it well.

This loaf should be crumbly and quite light.

CINNAMON TOAST

1 teaspoon ground cinnamon
3 teaspoons caster sugar
2 pieces hot buttered toast

Mix the sugar and cinnamon together and sprinkle on to the toast; eat straight away, hot and melting and spicy. Lovely for a winter tea.

For 2

MRS FITCH'S WALNUT BREAD

1 lb self-raising flour
1 level teaspoon salt
1 oz lard
4 oz walnut pieces
4 oz dates
3 oz sugar
1 egg
½ pint milk

Preheat oven to Reg 4½/185°. Sieve the flour and salt and rub in the lard. Chop the walnuts and dates and mix them into the rubbed flour together with the sugar. Beat the egg in the milk and mix it into the dry ingredients thoroughly, making a soft dough. You may not need all the liquid. Turn into a well-greased bread tin and bake in the oven for about an hour.

Allow to cool and butter the slices like ordinary bread. Very good for tea.

WALNUT OPEN SANDWICHES

Spread good fresh white or wholemeal bread with butter and cover with fresh (if possible) walnut halves. Sprinkle with a little coarse salt and eat. A few walnuts will go a very long way and they make a delicious elevenses.

MISCELLANEOUS

FRUIT SYRUPS

1 lb preserving sugar to 1 pint juice water

Put the fruit in a large china or earthenware basin with about ½ pint water to 3 lbs fruit and mash it down a bit with a wooden spoon or steak-beater. Stand the bowl, covered with a large lid, in a pan of water and put it in a slowish oven Reg 1/140° for one to two hours, mashing from time to time.

When the fruit seems to have softened as much as possible, take it out of the oven and strain it through a double muslin or jelly-bag, overnight if possible.

Next day add ¾–1 lb preserving sugar to each pint of juice, depending on how sweet you want the syrup. Add a little bag of cloves or cinnamon, or a dash of brandy or lemon juice if you like. Heat gently, stirring, in a large pan until the sugar is dissolved – no longer, or it will set like jam. Cool.

Have ready some small sterilised bottles, with sterilised screw caps (15 minutes in boiling water does the trick). Fill them with the syrup to within 1½–2 inches from the top and put on the screw tops. Without this space, the expanding hot liquid will burst the bottle when you sterilise it.

Stand the bottles in a deep pan with a false bottom, a pressure cooker is ideal, and pour in water almost to the top of the bottles. Bring the water to the boil and keep boiling for 20–30 minutes. Take out the bottles and stand them on a wooden table or on folded newspapers, not on a cold surface or they will crack.

When they have cooled tighten the screw tops if necessary and seal by dipping in melted wax, or with sticky tape.

Fruit syrup, as opposed to fruit squash, is incredibly expensive to buy and much nicer to drink. If there is a glut of any soft fruit such as blackberries, raspberries, blackcurrants, cherries, English grapes, strawberries etc., you can make your own. It will keep quite well until it is opened, after which it must be kept in the refrigerator.

It is very good in milk shakes or used as a sauce for a pudding, or of course as a base for a hot or cold drink.

CRABAPPLE JELLY

crabapples
water
sugar
bowl
tea-towel
string
jamjars
covers

You can flavour this with cloves, ginger or cinnamon. Pick out any unsound or bruised crabapples, and wash the rest well. Leave the stalks on, put in a saucepan and just cover with water. Simmer covered until they are a pulpy mass (about 30 minutes) prodding with a wooden spoon occasionally. Add the cloves, ginger of cinnamon now, if wanted.

Wet a clean tea-towel or similar cloth, in hot water and wring it out. Put it over a basin large enough to hold all the apple juice, pour the pulpy apples and juice into it, tie it tightly with string and hang it over the bowl on a convenient hook or nail. (Use the cup hooks on the dresser.) Let it drip about 12 hours.

Measure the liquid (it will be cloudy but never mind, it clears with the sugar), put it in a large pan and add 1 lb sugar per pint of juice., Stir over gentle heat until the sugar is melted. Then bring to a fierce boil, so it froths up high, which is why you need a large pan. Stir all the time, skimming, and test for jelling, by putting a little to cool on a saucer (when it wrinkles as you push it, it is ready) or when the drips are slow to leave the spoon if you hold it up over the pan. If you overboil, it will burn or go syrupy. If you underboil, it will be too runny and ferment. One pint can be ready in as little as ten minutes.

Pour into clean hot jam jars, which should be waiting in the oven. Cover when cold.

Very good eaten with sugared petit suisse.

SEVILLE ORANGE MARMALADE

10 good Seville oranges
2 lemons
10 lbs sugar (preserving sugar is best because it dissolves well, but granulated will do)
9 pints water
a muslin bag to cook the pips in

To make a year's supply for an average small family you need four times this amount, but 15 lbs is a convenient quantity to cook, providing you have a large preserving pan.

The oranges are only here for a short time in January but it really is worth making your own marmalade; it costs half as much

as shop marmalade and is twice as good. This method is spread over three days, but doesn't take much time on the second and third days.

1st day: halve and squeeze the juice from the ten oranges and two lemons. Sieve the juice to retain the pips. Shred the squeezed skins into large or small matchsticks, whichever you prefer, or if you are not fussy put them through the coarsest blade of your mincer. Pour eight pints of cold water over the peel and juice, and in a separate basin one pint of cold water over the pips. Leave to soak for 24 hours.

2nd day: strain the pips and put them in the muslin bag. Add their liquid to the peel and, in a preserving pan, simmer the pips with the peel very gently until the peel is quite tender. (Test by biting or by squeezing between finger and thumb). Do this in a pan with a lid; it takes about 1½ hours, but doesn't need watching or stirring. When tender leave the whole thing to soak another 24 hours.

3rd day: put fifteen clean 1 lb jam jars to heat in a low oven. Remove the bag of pips, pressing it to squeeze out all the juice which is an important source of pectin. Bring the marmalade to the boil in a large pan. Add the sugar, stirring well or it will burn. Boil very fast after the sugar has dissolved until setting point is reached, in 30–40 minutes. Test for setting by letting a little marmalade cool on a saucer or by holding up your spoon and waiting for the drips to become large, slow and heavy. Towards the end, take the pan off the heat while you wait for the results of the testing. Overcooking will produce a syrup that never sets, and undercooking produces a sloppy mess that won't keep, but this marmalade sets beautifully and keeps two or three years.

When it is absolutely ready, turn off the heat and allow to cool a little; it will soon start setting in the pan, so have your jars ready. Fill the jars, which should be standing on a board or newspapers, wipe them clean, allow them to cool and cover them carefully.

Makes 15 lbs

TOMATO KETCHUP

6 lbs ripe tomatoes
½ lb onions
½ lbsugar
1/8 oz paprika
pinch cayenne
1½ oz salt
1 fluid oz wine vinegar (chilli or tarragon)
spiced vinegar:
½ pint wine vinegar
small piece cinnamon bark
10 whole allspice
6 cloves
2–3 blades of mace
1–2 bayleaves
1 chilli pepper

Make the spiced vinegar: put the spices into the wine vinegar, bring it to the boil, take it off the heat and leave for two hours, covered. Then strain.

Slice the tomatoes and peel the onions; cook them covered until the tomato skins start to come away. Rub the pulp through a sieve, add sugar, salt, cayenne and paprika. Cook until the sauce thickens, then add the spiced vinegar and wine vinegar. Cook until the sauce thickens again to the consistency of thick cream.

Pour into hot bottles with sterilised tops and seal firmly. Leave to mature a month or two.

One pound of tomatoes makes about half a pint of ketchup, so this is only worth doing if you have masses of tomatoes and ready appetites for ketchup.

GERMAN GREEN TOMATO PICKLE

5 lbs green tomatoes, small enough to eat whole
2 pints cheap malt vinegar
1 ib white sugar
6 cloves, 1 inch cinnamon stick, and a piece of nutmeg or 2–3 blades mace (½ teaspoon powdered)
1 pint white wine vinegar
pinch salt

Remove the stalks from the tomatoes and put them, with their skins still on, in a large pan with the malt vinegar. Bring slowly to the boil, stirring. Then strain, put the tomatoes in a china bowl, and throw the vinegar away.

Bring the sugar, spices, wine vinegar and salt to the boil, stirring to dissolve the sugar, and pour it over the tomatoes. Leave in the bowl for 24 hours; next day, remove the tomatoes, boil up the liquid again, leave it to cool and pour it again over the tomatoes. Leave it for another 24 hours. The following day, bring the tomatoes and the liquid to the boil together, remove

the tomatoes, and reduce the liquid until it becomes slightly syrupy. Remove the spices. Put the tomatoes into clean hot jars, pour over the syrup, slightly cooled, cover and keep at least three months.

This takes three days to make and is ready to eat in three months. It is very sweet and delicious and looks beautiful, quite unlike anything you can buy at the grocer.

YORKSHIRE PUDDING

4 oz plain flour, salt
2 eggs, ½ pint milk
3 tablespoons oil or good dripping

Make the batter by sieving the flour and salt into a bowl, make a well in the centre and add the eggs, breaking the yolks with your spoon before you start stirring. Add the milk gradually, stirring in the flour little by little until half the milk is added; keep going until all the flour is taken up and the mixture is smooth. Then add the rest of the milk and beat for five or ten minutes. Stand the batter in a cool place for one hour. Preheat oven to Reg 9/240°. When the batter is ready, heat the oil or dripping in a baking tin, pour on the batter and cook five minutes at Reg 9/240° and 35–40 minutes at Reg 7/220°.

Batter to be made two hours in advance.

For 6

MELBA TOAST

Make toast in the usual way with slices of bread about quarter of an inch thick. Cut off the crusts and slice each piece of toast carefully in half through the soft centre, making two slices from one, each toasted on one side only. Turn the grill down to a moderate heat and toast the thin slices gently on their untoasted side. They will curl slightly, and should be served hot, in a crisp pile.

You can make this toast in advance and reheat in a low oven before serving.

HOME-MADE BREADCRUMBS

Collect all the left-over ends of loaves, making sure that none are going mouldy. Put them in a very low oven, or all day in the plate-warming drawer of your cooker, until they are completely dried and pale brown.

Lay a tea-towel on a firm table. Fold it neatly round the bread so that the crumbs cannot escape, and press a rolling pin all over it, crushing and crunching the bread. Hold a sieve over a baking tin and shake the crumbs through. Repeat the performance until the crusts are all fine crumbs. Store them in an airtight jar, and they will keep well.

MAKING FLAN CASES

Have some dried beans or spaghetti shells that you always use for flans. Keep them in a specific place and then the whole performance becomes miraculously easy. Throw them out every so often and start with fresh ones, as they develop a strong smell of burned flour which could transmit itself to the flan.

1. Preheat the oven to Reg 5/190°.

2. Butter a 7–8 inch flan tin with a loose bottom.

3. Roll out the pastry (page 146) to to ¼ inch thickness.

4. Line the flan tin with pastry lifted into place on the rolling pin. Trim the edges with a generous hand as the pastry does shrink.

5. Prick the bottom all over with a fork.

6. Line the flan case with a round piece of greaseproof paper.

7. Spill in the beans.

8. Put it into the oven for 15 minutes.

9. Take it out of the oven, remove the beans and paper.

10. Cook it a further ten minutes until the bottom is no longer soggy. It is now ready to be filled with a quiche mixture, apples or whatever you like and cooked in the normal way.

PLAIN PIE OR FLAN PASTRY

6 oz plain flour
1½ oz slightly salted butter
1½ oz cooking fat
½ teaspoon salt cold water

Sieve the flour and salt into a bowl. Chop the butter and cooking fat into it with a knife and then rub it in, lifting your hands several inches above the bowl with each movement, so that the fat is cooled by the air as it falls into the bowl; this may sound far-fetched but it really helps keep the pastry cool and therefore light. When it looks like fine breadcrumbs, carefully add water as you mix the pastry with your other hand until you have a light firm dough. Knead it together lightly, to distribute the moisture evenly. Stand it in a cool place, wrapped or covered, for at least an hour, before rolling out.

COCONUT ICE

2 lbs sugar
just over ¼ pint milk
1 oz butter
8 oz desiccated coconut
pink colouring

Put the sugar, butter and milk in a heavy saucepan and bring them slowly to the boil, stirring to dissolve the sugar. Boil for four minutes stirring all the time. Remove from the heat, add the coconut, stir well and pour half into a greased tin, one inch deep. Colour the other half and pour into a separate tin. Mark into fingers when it is half set, and cut when cool. It sets quickly so you should work fast. It is very good for Christmas presents and bazaars.

LEMONADE

5 lemons
1 ½ lbs granulated sugar
1 pint boiling water
½ oz citric acid

Thinly pare the lemons (no white) with a sharp knife or potato peeler, and pour one pint of boiling water on to this peel. Add the sugar and the juice of the lemons. Stir until the sugar dissolves, steep overnight and strain. Stir in the citric acid. Use diluted. This lemonade keeps for weeks in screw-top bottles in the refrigerator.

Makes 1 ½ pints concentrated juice

TO CLARIFY BUTTER

Clarified butter keeps better than ordinary butter and is used to seal up pates and home-made potted game and meat. It is also excellent for frying; it is the milk content in butter that makes it burn, and this is filtered out in the clarifying. It is also the nearest thing to ghee for making Indian curries.

It is not worth clarifying less than half a pound because you lose quite a lot on the way; more is worthwhile, since it keeps so well. Use the cheapest butter.

Melt the butter slowly in a thick saucepan, without browning. Turn off the heat, stir it and let it stand for a few minutes to settle. Line a sieve with a fine cloth squeezed out in hot water and stand it over a bowl. Pour in the butter and let it drip through. Allow to set and remove it from the bowl; pour away the water from underneath.

Clarified butter should be a lovely, even, semi-transparent yellow colour.

BEURRE MANIÉ

Mash together an equal amount of butter and flour and squeeze it in the palm of your hand to combine the two elements properly.

Use it to thicken stews and sauces at the end of the cooking.

CURE FOR INDIGESTION

Boiled water, drunk as hot as possible.

INDEX